TOP TIPS *to become a* MILLIONAIRE

Dr. Malik

MA Msc LLB JD

Solicitor

Foreword by

Dr. Philip Beresford

THE SUNDAY TIMES RICH LIST

This first edition is published in England, 2007

by DIRECTMILLION.COM

British Library Cataloguing in Publication Data

Malik, Akbar Ali
Top tips to become a millionaire
1. Entrepreneurship 2. Millionaires
I. Title
338'.04
ISBN-13: 9781873718155

Printed and bound in Finland by WS Bookwell.

directmillion.com
186 North End Road
West Kensington
London
W14 9NX
www.directmillion.com

To Raise Malik

"Go in peace; may luck attend you".

(ancient Greek saying)

Acknowledgements

Editor

Halima M. Malik

Art Director

Jason James

Chief sub-editor and assistant sub-editors

Vivienne DuBourdieu, Michelle Georgeson, Alison Batley

Contents

Preface

CONGRATULATIONS. By taking the initiative and buying this book, you have shown your determination and ambition. In fact, you've already taken the first step to becoming wealthy. You obviously want to learn how to make money and become wealthy. You don't need hundreds of pounds to get started on your road to making money. Even £10 is enough to get you started if you have the golden mind-set of a millionaire and seriously want to make money.

Perhaps you are already rich and want to make more money, or maybe you bought this book because you want to learn how to make money. Or maybe you are too embarrassed to ask how to make money.

Whatever your reason for forking out money to buy this book, or even borrowing it, well done. In this book you will learn some basic lessons about making money and putting yourself on the road to becoming a millionaire.

Remember that ancient Chinese saying, 'A journey begins with a single step'. You have to take that step if you want to succeed. Also, be clear from the outset that wealth comes from hard work, perseverance, a strong work ethic, and dedication.

Thank you for choosing to read this book. You have shown a serious commitment to create and generate wealth. There could be a variety of reasons you want to learn how to get rich. You too can become a millionaire. Believe in your power to generate wealth and you will.

You might think that to become a millionaire, you have to be born into a very rich family. This is untrue. There are hundreds of millionaires who were born into non-wealthy homes, but managed to become millionaires. Their stories are amazing and a lesson for all of you. They are true 'rags to riches' stories as we say in England and are good examples of what it means to be 'living the American dream'. You too can join that league.

Some people are scared of money. They think that to make money you need some advanced education or have knowledge of some special tricks. But this is completely untrue. You too can learn a few basic techniques to get you on the same road as other millionaires.

Wealth and success come to those who want them. You don't have to be 'born' rich. You can actually become rich or richer by learning a few techniques and getting into the right frame of mind. Apply the tips given to you in this book and I am positive that you will change how you perceive making a million pounds.

I have been a practising lawyer for over 25 years now and being a Solicitor and the CEO of an established law firm I have dealt with many millionaires and several billionaires. They each have their own life story to share. I have also met many people who have no wealth whatsoever. I am fascinated to learn everyone's story.

While writing this book, in my research and discussions with millionaires, I met a millionaire who was originally a T.V. presenter. He told me that by listening to what other millionaires 'say and do' he became a millionaire. Through observation he emulated the millionaires and eventually became one himself.

You don't necessarily need to be wealthy to have an excellent money-making idea. If you have a unique idea, you need to transform it into reality. Rome was not built in a day. You can dream and build imaginary castles, but you need to start putting the bricks down, one by one, as the building of every castle starts from a tiny stone or brick.

Another important bit of advice I can give you is to learn from other people, especially people who are older than you, especially your parents who can give you constructive advice about 'life'. Everybody can speak words of wisdom. It's up to you whether to listen or not. In Belgium there is a saying akin to 'experience is like a hair comb which life only presents you with when all your hair is gone'. So listen and learn.

One day I was walking past the laundrette opposite my office in East London and came across Mr Patel, the proprietor. I asked him jokingly "How is business are you making money?". Mr Patel looked at me and replied, "You can only make money if others make it for you". Encapsulated in these few words uttered by Mr Patel are precious words of advice. I agree with him. You will need other people to 'make money' for you.

In this book you will learn how to make money work for you and how to become rich. There are plenty of top tips to help you learn about the power of money. For those of you who haven't tried alternative therapies such as yoga, now is the perfect time. The large majority of millionaires I have spoken to have told me it's always difficult to make the first million pounds (or dollars). But after that making more millions is much easier.

You can learn to relax your mind and body. This in turn will help you think more positively and creatively essential keys for amassing wealth and becoming successful in all spheres of your life.

I wish you luck and good fortune on top of self-purpose and the willingness to persevere all the way in making your fortune. YOU CAN do it. You WILL achieve your goals. BELIEVE in your inner strength and dreams. Start your mission to make a million TODAY. There is absolutely NOTHING that can prevent you from achieving what you want.

I would like to say thank you to Dr Philip Beresford for contributing to the foreword of my book and his wise words. I would also say thank you to Sir Ghulam Noon, Lord Nazir Ahmad of Rotherham, Monika Singh and Bobby Dhillon, who provided thoughtful insights and support. I am indebted to Halima Malik, my colleague, for her untiring passion for my project and for editing the book. I wish also to say a special thank you to Jason James for art directing the book.

Thanks also to Maz, Kishan, Kamlesh Savaliya, and Sair Mir for their continued support, and to Martin Gill for his assistance in the proof-reading. I wish all my readers a blessed life journey filled with peace, happiness and continuing success.

Maybe, after becoming a millionaire, you too will still decide to chop wood and carry water!

Dr. Malik

London
April 2007

Foreword

By Dr. Philip Beresford
B.Sc (Social Sciences), M.Sc, PhD
THE SUNDAY TIMES RICH LIST

There is a story told among the bright and ambitious in the telecoms industry of one budding entrepreneur who saw a loss-making company advertised for sale at just £1 in the FT way back in 1989. He bought it, licked it into shape and the company is now worth over £260m, while the entrepreneur's stake is worth £156m and rising. Not a bad return on £1!

Tales of derring-do like this inspire and motivate the young and ambitious to go on their own personal journey to entrepreneurship, business building and ultimately, if they get it right, to "millionaire hood". Many of course try but sadly for them and for Britain not all succeed.

How do I know? Looking at Companies' House filings, we can see around 60,000 private and public companies which are the parent companies for around 1.7m subsidiaries in one form or another. Of these 60,000 there are 35,000 with directors who are shareholders either as families or founding entrepreneurs.

But only 9,000 of these are producing healthy profits of £1m or more which is the passport to wealth for the owner/owners as it would indicate by any rough and ready yardstick a company with a £10m or more valuation.

As a country we need to raise that percentage much higher by 50% at least, with all the attendant benefits in a higher tax yield and job creation that would follow as naturally as night follows day. Here it is heartening to report that the Asian business community is leading the way.

Looking at my database, built up over 18 years of compiling *The Sunday Times Rich List* and countless other industry and regional lists, I can report that while the overall proportion of self-made millionaires stands at an impressive 86%, within the Asian community it is a quite startling 97%.

Government recognises the need to drive entrepreneurialism forward to make the rest of Britain in a sense match the Asian community's success. Barely a day passes without the Chancellor and Prime Minister paying lip service to the cause of greater entrepreneurial spirit in the UK. Measures follow measures from government department to sponsor and nurture it. Business schools proffer MBA courses in entrepreneurship. TV programmes such as *The Apprentice* or *Dragon's Den* are also seeking to capitalize on the glamour now associated with the term entrepreneur.

Awards are sponsored by newspapers and leading entrepreneurs such as Sir Alan Sugar or Sir Philip Green are found in the gossip columns as much as the business pages. All this is brilliant if it makes the cause of starting a business seem attractive, taking the entrepreneur from his old image as a slightly seedy spiv dealing in dodgy gear (the Del Boy Trotter School of Entrepreneurship) into the 21st century.

Here he or she is seen as a business builder and a hugely powerful force in a global world where competitive markets freed from corruption, vested interests and the like are seen a cornerstone of a mature and thriving democracy. It is no accident, I would contend, that entrepreneurs thrive best in strong democracies and democracy flourishes in countries where entrepreneurs can thrive. The two are symbiotic in every sense.

So what does it take to become a successful entrepreneur and per se one of the lucky ones who runs a business making that magic Ł1m or more in profits which puts the owner on the route to becoming very wealthy indeed?

Firstly, and almost the most important factor, is where the potential entrepreneur was born? By this I categorically reject the notion that it helps to be born with a silver spoon firmly lodged in one's mouth, as the saying goes. Indeed inheriting wealth in any shape or form is usually a big disincentive to entrepreneurial activity.

The Asian community is a major exception here in its ability to inculcate business values from one generation to the next. But in the wider British society, if one has inherited a fortune, the odds of then creating another fortune or build on the first are no better than perhaps one in four.

And I say long may that stay like that. There is nothing more guaranteed to kill off enterprise than to have the higher reaches of business or society clogged up with a lot of clapped out, lazy deadbeats who have done nothing to earn their place or keep. We need the natural cull of capitalism to ruthlessly chop fortunes back when one generation can't succeed in carrying on a family business. It has to be taken over, grabbed by the private equity industry or the like and the family underperformers unceremoniously turfed out. If they have lost their fortunes, so be it.

It creates room for new entrepreneurs to come along and dominate the scene for a few years until their time is up, and a new group emerges. The constant refreshing of the entrepreneurial gene pool is vital. It means that all those aspiring at the bottom know that there is a chance they can make it that they can aspire to be the next Richard Branson or the like.

In this context it does help overwhelmingly and extremely perversely to be born dirt-poor. The poorer and harder one's early upbringing, the more one has to fight for life, the more determination one has, the more one gets used to the idea that nothing is given on a plate and it only comes with hard and unremitting toil. I have always been struck in this respect by the early years of Sir Anwar Pervez, recently named Britain's Master Entrepreneur of the Year for the way he has built up the huge Bestway cash and carry group here and developed large scale enterprises in Pakistan where he was born. Pervez, a farmer's son from Rawalpindi, walked several miles a day to school and several miles back. It was tiring, hot and yet he stuck at it knowing that education was the passport to a better future. And so it was to prove.

Pervez came to Britain at 21, and after working on the Bradford busses, opened his first specialist food shop in London in 1962, serving the Asian communities in west London.

Six years later Pervez opened his second shop which was a general grocery store for the people of south Kensington. From these early beginnings, he has built Bestway into a company with a £1.3 billion turnover and a fortune approaching £400m.

"Education, education, education" was Tony Blair's catchphrase that won him the 1997 landslide. But it is and has been vital for many from the Indian subcontinent to take them out of poverty. Indeed it could be said to be the secret weapon of the subcontinent in its economic drive, and the effect has rubbed off on the Asian immigrants and their offspring who have settled in Britain. I was struck by this when I recently received the newsletter from the Venkatraman Memorial Trust which I help support in a modest way. This trust helps schoolchildren in the poor fishing village of Kovalam in Tamil Nadu, south India. It was founded by a magnificently kind-hearted and energetic lady, Sylvia Holder, in memory of a lad called Venkat, whose education she had sponsored, after he was tragically killed in a road accident.

The newsletter in question reported a visit by one of the sponsors to the local school, with hardly any facilities. Yet she wrote: "For the first time in my life, all the children rose and politely said 'Good Morning'. I was struck by how smart all the children looked...."

But the Asian community here too can be a beacon of hope in education. I also know that from personal experience. My two sons, aged 12 and 14, go to a top-performing West London comprehensive, Drayton Manor. The headmaster, Sir Pritpal Singh, has been knighted for his achievements in turning a sink school into one that challenges and indeed surpasses some of the top-performing local private schools with its exam results.

From what my sons say, it is clear that the hardest- working students, those who listen intently to every word from the teacher in class without disruption, those who display the maturest attitude outside class by simply getting on with work quietly and without fuss, are largely drawn from the Asian community.

And yet, despite the need for better qualified people in an increasingly complex and much higher valued added economy that we have in Britain, the lack of education or the failure to do it can often be as much a spur in later life to a golden tomorrow as is being born in extreme poverty.

I know one property tycoon who when leaving school was told bluntly by his headmaster that he was useless and would achieve nothing. He was so angered by what he heard that he went on to build a £500m plus fortune. Another was similarly humbled by being handed a broom by his teacher as he was about to leave school, to be told: "Take this; it is all you are fit for." The man in question was so furious that he also went on to build a £100m fortune and took great delight a few years after leaving school to pass his former teacher (who was struggling on a bike) in his new Ferrari.

But the Ferraris do not come simply because one has experienced searing poverty and is determined to get out or through a seething rage at humiliation by failure at school. A supportive and loving family helps as Sir Richard Branson put it nearly twenty years ago: "My father and mother appreciated everything I was trying to do, encouraged me, and gave me lots of praise. This sets you off on the right footing to become the leader of a large company." It certainly did for Branson, who is now worth at least £3 billion on the back of the whole Virgin phenomenon.

Whatever one's background, making millions through business will not happen without the "big idea". It is vital to find that niche market that no-one else has attacked or thought up. Alternatively if a budding entrepreneur is determined to open the ninth corner shop on a street that has eight already, then his or her corner shop must be different and better in some way that the customer can see. It must have better products, a friendlier layout, offer home delivery, stock products that its customer ask for, get to nurture and hug its customers closely on almost first name terms, anything in effect that will give it an edge.

The budding entrepreneur knows this, as do a lot of non-entrepreneurs. But what sets him or her out from the crowd is their ability to make it happen. How many of us have sat in the pub with friends, family or workmates and on the third drink entered in a discussion which results in a really brilliant business proposition? Probably everyone has been there but only a tiny number have done it and seen it through. They are the true entrepreneurs who having developed a good idea take it through to execution and delivery. They are the eons who risk all by giving up a safe job to start out on their own, probably with a mortgage doubled to pay for the idea with the risk of losing the lot if it goes belly-up.

Their marriage will be on the line, as a partner may be worried about them throwing off security for the great unknown, and they will certainly not relish the long hours of stress and tension in the early days of building a business.

A good proportion of entrepreneurial marriages fail on this account. My tip here is to make one's partner in love a partner in business too it will help lessen the burden and make them appreciate what it is all about too.

As the entrepreneur's business grows, so will staff numbers. Staff are his or her lifeblood. It requires leadership of the highest calibre to be a good entrepreneur who can be likened to a successful general in this respect. He or she must be able to motivate staff, fire their enthusiasm for the job, make them want to work that little bit harder because they have huge pride in working for that entrepreneurial company.

Entrepreneurs also have a dogged determination to keep going when all normal human beings would have said to hell with it and packed up. Hamish Ogston, the man behind the card services group, CPP, slogged for a decade from 1980 to 1990 building his business when it recorded a loss every year. He refused to give up and eventually the business went into profit and Ogston is now worth in excess of Ⱡ400m on the back of its success.

James Dyson, now a household name for his vacuum cleaner, spent a total of fifteen years plugging away to get it on the market. In the five years from 1979 to 1984, he made 5,127 prototypes before he had perfected the design. It nearly bankrupted him and would drive mere mortals mad. But it was worth it. He is now comfortably a billionaire on the back of the profits rolling in to James Dyson Ltd.

Proud as a successful entrepreneur will be over his or her success and full of confidence too in the unique product or service that they can offer, none are blinded by this to the detriment of the business.

They can admit to mistakes, indeed the best entrepreneurs are the ones who spot their mistakes very early on, turn away from that path quickly (quick and decisive decision making is another classic trait of top entrepreneurs).

But above all, they learn from that mistake, take on board why and where they went wrong and make sure they never repeat it. Once bitten, twice shy is their motto in this respect.

Finally and above all in building that business and a passport to millionaire hood, the entrepreneur will remember day and night the old saying that "cash is king". He or she will watch the cash flow like a hawk, making sure that the money is coming in from customers, husbanding it carefully and paying out sparingly.

Many a seemingly successful entrepreneur has fallen by the wayside for ignoring cash flow until it is too late. Keeping the banks sweet is a necessary pain until that magic and delicious point arrives when the entrepreneur is so successful, has piled up so much wealth in the company or personally that the bank manager, formerly his or her master in every respect, comes crawling to them in the subservient role that banks should play. Many an entrepreneur has told me that that moment is the one they savour the most about their success.

And with that I leave you to read Dr. Malik's clear tips on a step by step guide on how to really succeed on the path to entrepreneurial success.

Dr. Philip Beresford

Chapter 1

What makes A Millionaire

I LOVE all those cartoons created by Joseph Barbera and William Hanna. They are absolutely fabulous. Barbera originally worked as a banker before turning his passion to creating cartoons. The films he created with his partner captured the attention of millions of people and are wonderfully made. They are classical masterpieces. I don't know if you ever watched them?

For those of you who haven't yet seen any Warner Bros Animation cartoons I strongly recommend you go out and watch some. There is one cartoon called Tom and Jerry. It's about a cat constantly chasing a mouse. There's the occasional scene where an image appears in the cat's eyes. Sometimes it could be food, but there's one scene I remember vividly. A dollar sign appears in each of the cat's eyes and this is accompanied by the sound of a cashier's till. It's just so funny; the cat thinks in one scene that he is rich. It's such a classic image and really does sum up the awe many people feel when they think of a million pounds. And my own personal definition of a millionaire is really the cat that got the cream! Warner Bros Animation is now worth billions of dollars!

Cartoons have indeed made millions for their founders. Just look at company Walt Disney, now a global household name. Walter Elias Disney was the brainchild behind this business. His story typifies what we mean by 'Living the American Dream'. Disney was a pioneer and a talented cartoonist who lived in Illinois and was one of five children. Born and raised on a farm, at an early age he discovered he could paint and draw. When he was older he left the farm for a new life in Hollywood with nothing in his pocket expect a few dollars and some of his artwork. His brother had some savings, a few hundred dollars and they put their money together and set up their project. Today the legacy of Walt Disney remains alive. The empire known as Walt Disney is now also worth billions of dollars.

When people think of generating a million pounds they tend to look for traditional routes other people have taken, for instance, shops, hotels, restaurants. There is absolutely nothing wrong in that - if the financial markets are buoyant money can be made. But there are whole areas where money can be made that have been neglected. Indeed many self-made millionaires have selected the not so traditional areas to make money and have become millionaires by pursuing their ideas. From selling packaged samosas' and offering door-to-door pampering to the stories of Walt Disney and Warner Bros companies. What they demonstrate is that turning your passion into a business can generate a billion dollar industry.

It's never too late to start your aim of becoming a millionaire. There is no age limit.

TOP TIP

YOU too can make a million pounds. YES, you can make that much money. In this book I will show you HOW to do that. But let's start first with a definition of what is a millionaire. This will help you appreciate what you are aspiring towards and what it means to be a millionaire. After all if you are going to become one you need to be aware of what that means. *The Collins Dictionary* defines a millionaire as “a person whose assets are worth at least a million of the standard monetary units of his country”. *The Oxford Dictionary* defines a millionaire as “a person possessing a million pounds”. One thousand thousand equals a million. For the purpose of this book we are excluding millionaires who own one thousand thousand currencies other than the pound or dollar due to current economic global monetary exchange rates.

There are different 'types' of millionaires. Some millionaires own more than £1 million. For those who are not millionaires, a millionaire appears to be a very lucky person indeed. Often the public perception of what is a millionaire is influenced by what they see, read and hear in the popular press, TV and movies. The millionaire 'lifestyle' as perpetuated by the media is often glamorous, lavish and A-list. They are constantly followed around by the paparazzi, shown shopping at exclusive designer shops, driving outlandishly expensive cars and normally have a large entourage in tow to meet their everyday needs. They dine at top-notch expensive restaurants and jet around the world in their private planes and yachts, partying and holidaying in sensational holiday resorts.

They often are seen to own a plethora of homes in major cities around the world with personal chefs and butlers and stationed at each. Their stylists advise them to buy clothes, accessories, shoes - all designer labels of course! Such ideas capture the popular imagination.

Is this your idea of millionaires? Indeed many millionaires do live this lifestyle - money can after all buy luxuries beyond belief. But there are also millionaires who do not live such extravagant lifestyles.

Millionaires possess different personalities and have different aspirations in life, as we shall see later in the book. Some millionaires enjoy being in the 'public eye' and the public status that is attached to their wealth. They need to show their wealth to increase their standing and reputation. Certainly many millionaires can live this lifestyle that their fortunes afford, but at the same time, many choose to live more private lives.

Find a role model and emulate them.

TOP TIP

There are many different ideas of how millionaires 'live their lives'. Have you ever thought about what you would do if you won a million pounds? The first thoughts that would spring to most minds would be the expensive holidays, homes and clothes they could purchase. But what of the long-term future? What would you do once you had spent all the million pounds? Surprisingly it's not difficult to spend such an amount.

People have managed to spend vast sums in just a few months or blow it all in a matter of years!

Unbelievable you may think, but it has happened. Just read some of the stories of millionaires who won the lottery and you will note how many spent it all in a short space of time, to be left with absolutely nothing - literally no money, no home and even no friends. What made them blow all their money quite so freely? How did this happen? Often it is down to the fact that these over-night millionaires have had no previous exposure to wealth and when they won the money it was difficult to cope with it. Indeed it was a shock for many.

I love the following words by Jeffrey Archer in his book *'Not A Penny More, Not A Penny Less'* (published by Hodder & Stoughton): "Making a million has always been difficult. Making a million illegally has always been a little easier. Keeping a million when you have made it is perhaps the most difficult of all". Making money illegally is disingenuous and is contrary to the natural laws of the universe. The methods you use to generate wealth have their own implications. There is nothing better than earning and generating wealth through your own hard work - rewards are definitely sweeter. Maybe this could go some way to explaining the great splurge of lottery winners.

So think carefully before you set off on your mission to make a million pounds. You obviously need a strategy, a workable plan. There are several key ingredients that a self-made millionaire needs and I will reveal these secrets within this book. If you can follow the tips and advice given diligently, I am certain that you will become rich. This is not a pipe dream you can make it a reality.

For some people acquiring a million pounds seems like an impossible task. That is the sure way to fail in your mission to become wealthy. You have to BELIEVE you CAN make money.

If you think like a failure you will become one - it's as simple as that. That is another basic universal law.

This is a fertile time to make money.

TOP TIP

Successful people tend to possess a completely different mind-set. A POSITIVE mind-set will help you on your way to becoming rich.

In this book I will be concentrating on self-made millionaires. A self-made millionaire (often first generation) is a UNIQUE creature. He/she generated and created their own wealth in their own lifetime. They did NOT inherit the million pounds, but made their first million though their own strong work ethic. Indeed many self-made millionaires have gone on to become billionaires. In the course of doing so, they have inspired the new generation of 'wannabe millionaires' to use them as role models and aspire to their status. Their stories show that fortune and wealth is not just the preserve of a select few.

Historically, there has never been a more fertile time to become rich as there is right now. How is that possible? The world is indeed becoming SMALLER. Global markets are emerging all over the world and are also much more easily ACCESIBLE than they were previously. For instance there is now the worldwide web, which allows businesses to advertise their goods, meetings can be done virtually, information can be shared quickly.

Because of this rapid mass communication, international globalization, and information technology, the dream of amassing wealth globally is not simply a pipe dream but a reality for many. Nowadays you don't even need to buy a literal shop to trade. Many successful companies have learned the power of internet retailing and are using it to amass money.

One key principle applied by all these self-made millionaires is INVESTMENT. That is the key to not only acquiring wealth but also holding on to it and generating even more wealth. Whether it's investment of time, money, efforts, passion, it is the crucial underlying factor to the success of many self-made millionaires.

Others have used their gut instincts to pursue their dreams - their sixth sense, meaning the power of their own inner energy, to follow through with a project or idea that resulted in the creation of wealth.

Remember Rome wasn't built in a day

TOP TIP

Having conducted my own research it is clear that a significantly large proportion of self-made millionaires do not act out a lavish and extravagant lifestyle. Instead they lead a comfortable lifestyle, buying the occasional treat or goods and continue to invest thereby accumulating more wealth. Those self made millionaires whose assets are now worth millions, or more than a million, can afford to buy luxury goods and enjoy themselves - and why shouldn't they? They earned it.

Remember, sometimes the first million pounds (or dollars) is not made in one year, but over a period of years. Once that target is achieved, it can be doubled and turned into millions. To some people this may seem like a dream that will never come true. But let's break it down into a digestible format for those who cannot conceive the nature of wealth.

When you have 1p, you probably know that through some hard work or bargaining you can turn that 1p into 100p (making £1). Now imagine turning that £1 into £10. How would you do that?

Go further. Imagine that £10 becoming £1,000. Then imagine that £1,000 turning into £10,000. Continue this visualization, and you will have the ability to grasp how 1p can turn into a million pounds.

Chapter 2

Positive Energy Creates Abundance

When you think of money what do you see? Tangible notes, coins? Ultimately money is 'energy' and nothing more. It is worthless on its own. Money only becomes a powerful weapon when the financial and economic markets back it up. The poorer your country, the less value your currency will hold in the global market.

The more economically powerful the country in which you live, the better chances you have of accumulating substantial wealth and achieving your dream of becoming rich. I use the term 'rich' simplistically in this context. You can be rich in many different things, but for now I mean 'money' or 'wealth'.

Did you know that the universe is actually a hotbed of energy? Did you also know that you could actually TAP INTO THIS ENERGY and USE it to create and generate wealth? If not, then I will tell you how you can use the energy around you to help you on your journey to making a million pounds. You DON'T have to believe in magic or superstition to use the techniques of two ancient disciplines to help you along. These disciplines I am writing about are known as feng shui and vastu.

They are not magical formulas or magical pills and potions. They are basically two systems used for thousands of years by people in China and India to generate wealth. Traditionally they were jealously guarded and protected and the secrets of these sciences were only revealed to a select few because of the fear the systems would be used and abused for the wrong purposes. Today however, I am going to explain to you what they mean. You can then apply them to your own lifestyle and effect positive changes within your own life.

You CAN improve the SUCCESS and PROSPERITY in your home, business and personal life by applying principles of feng shui and vastu. Feng shui literally means 'wind' 'water'. Vastu means dwelling and is essentially the art of placement/design. Both are used to manipulate energy in the environment to encourage the positive flow of energy. This energy can help you ATTRACT (amongst others) wealth, love and prosperity.

Practitioners of feng shui and vastu work with the basic laws of the universe. If you want a major revamp it's best to consult an expert in these fields, otherwise you could actually create negative energy and that's not what you need. There are however some basic tips you can incorporate into your daily life to help you tune into the environment and yourself.

"A journey begins with a single step" (Chinese proverb)

TOP TIP

There's also another very good reason to learn some feng shui/vastu. If you are on a mission to make a million, and hopefully you will have a thriving business in the years to come, you will DEFINITELY need good quality staff and a harmonious, safe environment in which they can work and your customers can visit. You can encourage good business relationships with customers simply by changing the environment.

The Chinese have been using feng shui for centuries to encourage successful love relationships, increase wealth, reduce stress and enhance domestic bliss. Feng shui principles were used primarily in the formulation and planning of burial sites. The ancient Chinese considered death a momentous occasion. Therefore, the place where the Emperor and other nobility were buried was meticulously chosen. Mountains and water near the burial site were considered auspicious.

The discipline of feng shui is used to describe man's relationship with his environment. A naturally balanced environment where aspects such as objects, furniture, colours, and design are properly placed and planned can, according to ancient Chinese thinking, produce remarkable effects for the mind, body and the spirit.

In feng shui practice, we work with the flow of qi (pronounced 'chi') energy. Almost all spiritual traditions work with energy and have devised techniques to help improve the quality of qi. The ancient Indians also formulated their own techniques to help the flow of positive energy in their environments. That discipline is known as 'vastu'.

It is unsurprising that the ancient Indians and Chinese had similar ideas, as geographically they are neighbors, so it seems logical that ideas would filter between the two civilisations. Whether feng shui or vastu was the first discipline remains debatable. What is clear though, is that individual's centuries ago understood and appreciated the significance of energy and realised that it had the potential of affecting their environments (both the inner landscapes of the mind, body, and spirit) and outer landscapes (their home and workplace).

Use Feng Shui to attract wealth

TOP TIP

In feng shui practice, energy known as chi or qi is considered either to be 'sheng' (good energy) or 'sha' (negative energy). Often described in feng shui parlance as poison arrows, sha qi is believed to create bad luck, misfortune and ill health. Our aim is to attract free flowing sheng qi into your environment. In this respect, practitioners use a wide range of techniques. A compass is popularly used to isolate the directions of your room. Each direction has its own, unique energy frequencies. Appropriate objects are then placed in the room to help the energy move freely and simultaneously create peaceful and auspicious effects for the inhabitants of that room.

There are different ways you can work with energy. Feng shui practitioners have a choice of working with different styles. Popular styles of feng shui include the Compass School, Five Element theory, the Pa Kua method, and the Pa-chai (8 directions) school. For the moment suffice to be aware that there are different techniques. Underlying all these styles is the aim of working with energy to create positive results.

Just think - a dirty, smelly, cluttered kitchen, bathroom, bedroom, or office will definitely generate bad 'vibes'- do you really believe customers like filthy environments think again if you do. You will lose customers if you don't keep your shop/office reasonably clean. Some of the most successful companies have attracted customers simply by changing their environments. They have increased the morale of their staff by giving them a beautiful environment to work in, thereby increasing productivity and good relationships.

A dirty, cluttered, dark, or dingy environment is unlikely to attract prosperity. Nor will it have any positive effects on your state of mind. The ancient Indians and Chinese were masters at the art of creating harmonious environments.

Feng shui practitioners use many different techniques from varying disciplines. They include art, interior décor, design, astrology, gemology, and geomancy. Natural landscapes have been accepted by almost all traditions and disciplines as being extremely auspicious, and in feng shui the closer your environment is to nature, the better the quality of qi.

Feng shui really does offer something for everyone. It can help the stressed-out student who wants to improve his or her concentration and motivational powers, or the busy executive who wants to relieve tension and improve

Learn to work with the energy field that surrounds you.

TOP TIP

productivity. It can even be used to improve sexual and marital relationships. Does all this sound too good to be true? Well, whether the possibility of these things surprises you or makes you curious, my advice is to test it out for yourself and measure it by the results you get. Feng shui has moved a long way from its humble origins and is now big business. Commercial corporate environments, including some of the biggest names in the City, have used feng shui to change their working landscapes with spectacular results. For instance, where meeting and boardrooms with oblong/ rectangular tables were once the norm, they are now being replaced with round ones to avoid conflict, confrontation and ego trips.

Feng Shui is not magic; you have to use your common sense in applying it. Therefore there's no point in rushing out to fill your shopping bags with the talismans and ornaments recommended by feng shui practitioners if the environment in which you place them is not yet ready to work with them. The same principle applies to the body. There's no real point in spending an hour on yoga exercises, only to follow it with a big, fast-food meal full of artificial colourings, additives and sweeteners, and chasing it down with a couple of glasses of lager.

In feng shui, when you take out at least an hour to polish up and clean your environment of dirt, clutter and filth, and then place your talismans or ornaments appropriately, you will help the energy to move more quickly and beneficially. In yoga there is a concept known as the chakras (energy centers).

These energy centers are located in the body and can be accessed by using a variety of exercises. When the chakras are active and energy is flowing through them freely, the practitioner will feel energized and positive. In the same way as your body flows with energy, your environment has its energy points. If you view your environment as a dead entity, it will be difficult for you to attune to and integrate with. But when you perceive it as a live and active being, you will definitely become more at one.

As your awareness levels increase, which can be helped especially if you already work with energy, in the form of practicing a martial art or yoga, then you will begin to feel energy not only within you, but also around you and your environment.

Aside from feng shui (and its similar counterpart vastu), there are other disciplines, which can be used to help in generating wealth. Many millionaires I have spoken to also use astrology and gemstones. This is prevalent in the Indian sub-continent where many people believe in the

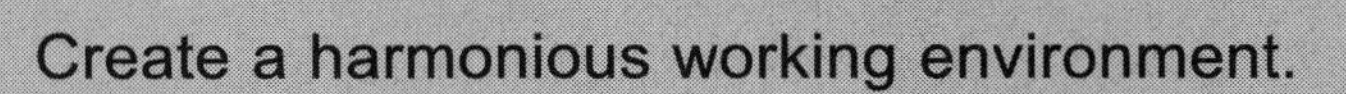
Create a harmonious working environment.

TOP TIP

magical power of gems. A large majority of people also believe in Vedic astrology and charter the course and movements of planets and stars. Whether these disciplines work or not depend on trial and testing, but I do know of several millionaires who regularly wear particular gems as talismans.

You may also wish to explore the subject of Vedic astrology. There are certain auspicious times during the year, month, day when it is beneficial to start new projects or deal with certain business and wealth related matters. The waxing moon phase for instance is not a good time to start new projects.

Every living thing is comprised of energy. Gems have their own intrinsic energy vibrations. You must have felt the serenity and calm of a natural lake, river, or even a stream of water. The beauty and stillness of an open countryside may have filled you with inspiration. Therefore, your environment is highly significant. It defines who you are, and where you are. It is a mirror of your being. Count the hours you spend on a daily basis in your office, and in your home.

The environment in which you live and work impacts strongly on your psychology - it definitely affects your mental state. The colours, the shapes, and the furniture almost everything in that environment leaves their impact on you, whether you believe it or not.

As we discussed earlier, an unpleasant or cluttered environment can be demoralizing. Even more importantly, it can exacerbate stressful conditions and increase tension, leading to a vicious circle of irritability and conflict.

You can enhance the peacefulness and calmness in your environment by using a few of the following simple techniques. To create an auspicious, harmonious environment, qi must be allowed to flow freely. Stagnated qi can lead to illness and bad fortune.

Moreover, it affects the emotions negatively. However and here's the crunch unless you have a nice healthy bank balance, you can't normally start from scratch. This does not mean, of course, that you cannot apply some basic feng shui techniques to help you succeed.

So, have you begun to wonder what little things you can do to change the course of qi in your personal environment? Here are a few tips to get you started, and to prevent sha qi from attacking your home or workspace.

Stagnated qi (energy) can lead to bad fortune.

TOP TIP

Be cable conscious

Box up any electrical equipment, including electrical wiring ask any good DIY store for help or contact a carpenter who can do a tailored job for you.

Sharp pointed objects

Remove sharp pointed objects from your environment; these are unnatural and cut into free-flowing qi. These might include angular, upward-pointing ornaments.

Green and clean

Put out withered and dying plants. These sap energy and obstruct its natural, harmonious flow.

Dust free living

Clean and dust regularly. Any build-up of dust can attract negative energy and affects your health.

In the round

Substitute rectangular, square and hard-edged tables with round ones, otherwise the shape will cut into the free-flowing qi. A round table is also more conducive for business meetings.

Drape over

If you have bookshelves, smooth off their pointed, angular ends, or drape cloth over to stop them generating 'poison arrows' (sha qi).

They have to go

Remove pictures that show violent, unsettling scenes. These not only send negative vibrations out into your environment, but can also be unsettling for other people.

Mirror mirror on the wall

Remove paintings and hanging mirrors off the wall if they are next to your bed, or on a wall behind your desk, as these can be unnerving and foster an element of surprise.

A round table as opposed to one with harsh straight lines can be more conducive to business meetings.

TOP TIP

Someone's behind you

If your desk faces away from the office door, and your back is to it, try and change the orientation of your seating otherwise it engenders insecurity.

Break it up

Avoid straight lines in your environment, including the shape of rooms, walls, windows, or shutters, as all angles can help to prevent the free flow of qi. You can break up the straight lines by introducing hanging crystals and ornaments or using soft upholstery and curtains.

Bed knobs and broomsticks

Don't place your bed opposite a door. This will affect your health as the qi flows in and is obstructed. Place your bed next to the wall to give an added feeling of security.

Brighten up

Use lamps to create ambience and enhance your mood. In the winter season make sure you receive plenty of light. Deprivation of light can significantly affect your moods negatively.

Mix-up

Break up the elements. For instance, if you have a wooden table, add to the beauty of that element by placing a silver candelabrum on top.

Scent up

Use fresh pot-pouri in bowls in bedrooms and other rooms to create a fragranced environment. You can buy many different shapes of bowls and colours to help cheer you up and to help you think with clarity.

Sleepless nights

Use natural cotton on beds, preferably in whites and creams. You can drape bedspreads over for added beauty and comfort. If you prefer use another type of material but try and keep it natural.

Creating illusions

Use wardrobes with mirrors to create space but don't sleep in front of them, it creates negativity, hence the connection to bad luck.

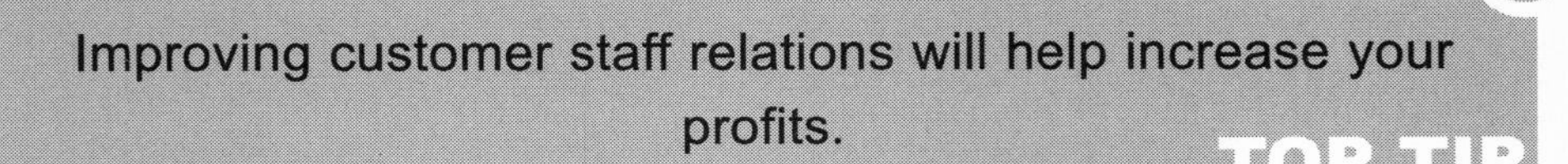

Blinded

If you opt for blinds, use wooden ones, as they are more in keeping with nature. Any other type can cut into your environment.

Your empire

Read how you can strengthen and improve not only the quality of your own energy but also that of your environment. When these principles are applied to your work environment, especially if you are trying to make money, you will be surprised at the financial results that can be achieved.

When you run your own business, invest some money into improving your environment. It doesn't need to be a huge amount. Your investment here will help generate interest in your office, shop, etc. Hopefully, it will also improve customer staff relations, which in turn will have a knock-on effect with your profits.

Remember that it's your customers or clients who will make or break your bank balance. If you are running a business and have inefficient, rude, untrustworthy, obnoxious staff, just remember you are losing money invisibly. For instance, customers will go elsewhere to your competitors. If you want to make money in business you need trained staff, who know how to treat customers and clients with courtesy. Just because you have a customer now doesn't mean that he will always be your customer.

A few key tips on how to apply some of these techniques are listed below. To rejuvenate your environment, to help you think clearly and positively use any of the following ideas:

Plants

Jade money plants are good for attracting wealth. Similarly, bonsai trees have always been adored by the East both for their special spiritual significance, and for their ability to attract good energy.

Mirrors

You can hang mirrors to create the illusion of space, especially in small box-rooms or dark areas of the house. But make sure you don't hang one over your bed, as it will give you a feeling of unrest. One excellent place to hang a mirror is above your dining room table, especially when you have food laid out. It doubles the effect and attracts good vibes.

Candles

These come in many different colours and varieties. In the bedroom, use red, orange, and maroon as these signify passion, love, and romance. White candles can be used in the dining area, and are a sign of spiritual energy. However don't light candles in reception areas unless your business is designed for pampering i.e. salons, spas etc.

Animal ornaments

Favoured by the Chinese, turtles are auspicious and symbolize good luck. Ornaments in the shape of a dragon or phoenix can be placed for good luck. Lions and doves are also auspicious symbols to place about the home.

Gems

Jade is highly favored. Place gems, or ornaments cut from gems, around your environment to help attract positive energy. Examples of appropriate gems are ruby, emerald, and the many different varieties of crystals, which can be bought at reasonable prices.

Wind chimes

These come in many different sizes and are made from a variety of materials. Hang them outside your window or indoors to attract positive energy. The beautiful sound of wind chimes also help good energy flow.

Water features

These help dispel negativity and sluggishness in your environment.

UV filters

Use these on computer screens to prevent the generation of negative electrical vibrations, and to protect your face and eyes.

Flowers

Lotus flowers symbolise love, peace, and spirituality. Roses are reminiscent of love and grounding. There are hundreds of different types of plants and flowers you can use in your home, office and gardens.

If you are running a business and have inefficient, rude, untrustworthy, obnoxious staff, just remember you are losing money invisibly.

TOP TIP

Crystal bowls and vases

Crystals have long been known for their powerful healing effects. Spiritual healers throughout the centuries have loved their intrinsic healing energy. Even contemporary modern science has confirmed that crystals do indeed have their own intrinsic energy vibrations.

You can purchase hanging crystals for windows and ornaments that are cut from crystal. Try amethyst and clear quartz. Smoky quartz can be placed on desks.

Fish bowls and goldfish

A small goldfish bowl with two goldfish in it is a sign of wealth and attracts positive energy.

Bowl of coins or conch shell

You can place one of these in your office to help attract wealth.

ColourTherapy

The effect of colour on our emotional well being and health has been explored and tested for decades. In the ancient Indian yoga traditions, working with colour to help strengthen the mind and body has been extensively used, particularly in the *Kundalini* yoga tradition. The use of colour therapy can also be traced to such ancient civilisations as the Egyptians, Greeks, and Chinese.

There are many different techniques used in colour therapy and in yoga. For instance, the use of gems can help strengthen the energy centres (*chakras*). Colour therapy can also be used effectively to help create and generate wealth. It can also be used to help you think creatively and even improve your general overall well being.

Feng shui practitioners often make use of colour. They will often advise on the types of colours to use in your home colours that complement your lifestyle and help to encourage auspicious events. It is a positive practice to use the colours red and pink in bedrooms as they are thought to encourage love and passion, while green and blue are used for healing and soothing.

Colour therapy can be used to help generate wealth. Green and gold are auspicious colours.

TOP TIP

Throughout the world, we can find examples of how people use colour to enhance the quality not only of their physical and mental states, but also their spiritual nature. For instance, in many traditions white robes are worn because the colour is linked to spiritualism, innocence, and higher truth. Places of worship also use colour to help induce a sense of healing and tranquility.

Colour therapy is known to help sufferers overcome depression, heal pain, and to induce a tranquil and healing environment. Countless studies have shown how colour affects our emotions and our ability to express ourselves. This method of healing can be used safely alongside traditional orthodox medicine.

Rainbows too are not the stuff of fairytales but mark real events, occurring daily. A rainbow is a band of colours created by light, and light is intrinsically energy. Individuals experiencing severe depression, or with SAD (seasonal affective disorder) are frequently encouraged to incorporate the colour yellow into their lifestyles as it has an uplifting effect on the mood.

Chapter 3

Tapping Into The Power of Your Subconscious Mind

IT IS TIME to examine synergy, which means the mutually advantageous coming together of different elements. A synergistic approach successfully assists people to live in peace and harmony with themselves and others, and to create balanced lives filled with unlimited possibilities. Tapping into synergy is an important step in accessing the power of your mind. And remember, you are tapping into the power of your mind in order to get rich.

As you have probably realised, you are what you believe. That means there is nothing more important than your self-confidence. If you hold a job and people try to put you down don't let it affect you. Stop worrying about what others think of you. Remain calm and detached and try to avoid the company of those who are negative. At the same, time if your manager is giving you constructive advice take it and learn.

Your mind, and the direction in which it is focused, can either make or break your ability to succeed in any field of endeavour. It is an extraordinary and brilliant machine. If you want to make money don't complain that you are too busy to make money. Tell yourself instead the key is to make time to make money.

Does it surprise you to know that the power of the mind can directly affect how much money you make, whether you will succeed in accumulating wealth, or become happy, prosperous, healthy, and confident?

Yes, in order to make money you must believe that you can do it. You need to access and program the subconscious mind. This is an ancient yogic technique, which works on two levels of the mind: the conscious and the subconscious.

The conscious mind is the rational, logical side of the mind. It controls our day-to-day activities. Think of a computer, with the subconscious mind as the hard drive. It feeds and sends signals to the conscious mind (the computer screen).

If you feed the subconscious mind with negative thinking, then ultimately it will program itself to believe it is so. Do you ever tell yourself 'I am useless', 'I will never be wealthy', 'I can't achieve my goals', 'I am not happy'? These entire messages become stored in the subconscious, and therefore your mind begins to accept and believe these statements.

Ultimately, it will direct these to the conscious level where these directions will become evident in your day-to-day activities. Studies show that patients recovering from

> You can become a millionaire by tapping into the power of your mind.
>
> **TOP TIP**

illness recovered much more quickly when they believed that they would.

You have to learn to feed the subconscious mind daily with positive statements. Eventually, through repetition, they will sink in and your conscious mind will live the reality of the words. But you have to believe that you will succeed, become rich, be happy. If you are only 50% sure of this, then you are wasting your time. Learn to use your mind to generate wealth.

Imagine if someone held a gun to your head and told you that you had only 24 hours to make £10,000, otherwise you would be shot. I am confident that you would give it your best shot. Your mind may even be on higher alert than normal and the results produced would, in all likelihood, be of a high quality. Perhaps you may even tap into creative thinking powers that you never thought possible. Whilst this may seem like a rather far-fetched scenario, the point I am sure has not been lost.

You have to think rich to become rich. Control the mind and unleash your hidden powers. You should become familiar with your thought processes, and not treat them as if they were random processes. What you act out on a daily basis is often a result of your conditioning. Apply the skills that help you make money to other areas of your life, including your health and personal relationships.

What people say to you, and who you were brought up to be, will affect you as you grow into adulthood. Perhaps you grew up in a family where you experienced a high level of poverty. You may have become conditioned to either hate or love money.

There are numerous success stories of millionaires who grew up in humble and poverty-stricken surroundings it was their belief and their ambition to make money that fuelled their success. These beliefs kept them striving until they achieved their goal. Admirably, they practically programmed themselves into believing that they could not only rise above poverty, but also make money and enjoy the luxuries that wealth brings. Nonetheless, they realised that to achieve that aim they had to overcome any obstacles that were placed in front of them. Our minds are strange things. They can break or make us.

To start any business of making money you need to have certain key traits, including confidence in your abilities. If you are feeling depressed, and in a negative frame of mind, this will present major obstacles on the road to making money. So be positive in outlook and enjoy what

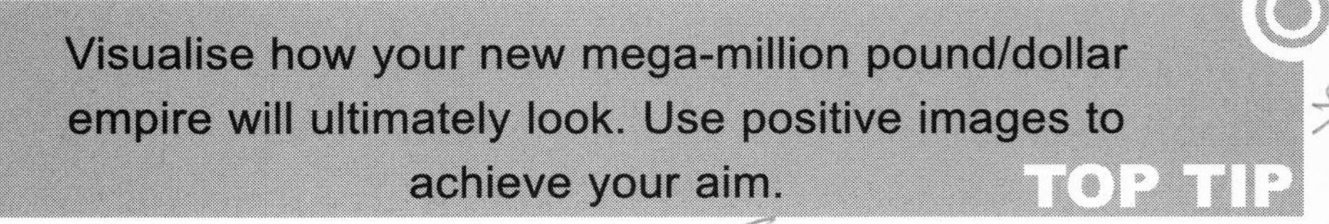

you are doing. Even when you feel like giving up, tell your mind that you can keep on going.

Sometimes when you are looking for funding for your project set-up you may be nastily turned down by the bank but that shouldn't stop you from persisting in your dream. Be sure you are absolutely sure that you have a viable business idea and there is an audience for it.

Aside from banks there are other methods of raising initial set-up costs, for instance someone else may want to come in as a partner who contributes a certain percentage to the business in return for a cut of the profits - maybe someone from your family or a friend. Some foundations such as the Princes Trust offer start up loans and some EC funding may be available for your projects especially if it may benefit your local community so keep your eyes open.

Learn to take out some time during the day to constantly affirm to yourself that you will succeed, that you are successful, and loved. Over a short passage of time, you will notice that you are beginning to attract the right vibes and becoming successful. Take control of your life now and you will see dramatic results unfold. Don't take my word for it. Try it, and see the difference.

Also learn to meditate. This will greatly improve your powers of concentration and stamina. Positive visualisation is formulating pictures of the future, envisioning yourself as being rich. To make money, not only do you need to believe in your own inner power to create and make more money, you need to visualise abundance. Look around you, there are millions of pounds flying around. They may not literally be in front of your eyes, but they are definitely all around you, albeit filtering on masse through the banking system, or via the unfailing march of money through tills.

What you need to do is tap into this, and find out how you too can make that money out there work for you. When you are starting up a business and you have a savings shortfall, where will you raise the extra cash? The bank would be an obvious answer. But you have to learn to access that money; otherwise you won't actually get yourself on the road to riches. If the bank rejects you for a loan, where will you go next? Do you have any other sources of income? Is there anyone else you could turn to?

If you have money, even if it's only a small amount, you can work on doubling its value. How? Through a second job, to start with, and through saving once you have mastered the expertise of investing it.

Aside from banks, take a look around for other potential sources for help to start up your business, for instance EC funding or a partnership with a like minded person. **TOP TIP**

Psychologically, you need to convince yourself that you are worthy of receiving money. Unless you make that affirmation, it is unlikely you will ever make any money. When you believe in your worth, you can convince others of your worth. So if you have self-doubt, fear, or a lack of confidence, you need to work on releasing these negative emotions.

You could start by making some chill-out time every day to work on improving your body strength and for releasing tension from the mind. Remember, you don't have to work yourself into the floor, or let your health suffer as result of working to make money.

Your mind, body, and spirit are three critical elements that will help you on the road to success. It is a fundamental rule that if you are in poor health, your mind and your consciousness are afflicted with negative energy. In turn, this will directly affect whatever project you are working on. The ancient civilisations were well aware of the power of energy and how it could be used beneficially for self-development.

The subconscious mind is your filter. Whatever you put in there is your mind-food. This will be reflected in your daily actions. You can use self-hypnosis to train the sub-conscious mind to help you grow rich. Think positive thoughts before you lay down to sleep. These thoughts will imprint themselves into your mind during your sleep. When we sleep we go into a deep trance like state.

Hypnosis has worked to change the habits and addictions of people. It has proven to be an excellent therapy and it works. Basically with hypnosis you are changing your subconscious mind. It is a therapy that really works if carried out safely and effectively.

I remember watching one of Paul McKenna's shows a while back. He took a random person and told him to count from 1 to the number 6. The man did as Paul asked counting "1, 2, 3, 4, 5, 6".

Then Paul put this man into a hypnotic trance and told him during that state that he would now forget the number 3. The man was asked to repeat the numbers and count from 1 to 6, but no matter how hard he tried he just could not remember the number 3. When the man was taken out of the trance he was asked to count from 1 to 6 again. This time he remembered perfectly the number 3.

Then there was another scene where Paul McKenna gave a random man from the audience an onion and put him into a trance state. He made suggestions to the man

Learn to meditate. This will greatly improve your powers of concentration and stamina.

TOP TIP

that the onion was an apple and it was delicious. The man because he was in a trance ate the onion happily and enjoyed it because he thought he was eating an apple. When the man was taken out of his trance he was shocked to see that he had in fact eaten an onion!

If you are planning to visit a hypnotist, as opposed to self-hypnosis, make sure you check their credentials. Paul McKenna is a famous hypnotist and his practical exercises are done in a safe and confined space.

I have outlined 2 auto-hypnosis exercises that you can practise:-

Exercise I - Positive Visualisation

One simple auto-hypnosis exercise you can do before you go to bed is as follows:-

- Relax and ensure that you will not be distracted by anybody.
- Lay down on your back and inhale deeply and then exhale deeply. Take at least 10 deep inhalations and 10 exhalations.
- Feel your whole body relaxing.
- Imagine you are clearing out your mind. Continue inhaling and exhaling long deep breaths.

- It may be difficult for you to let-go of all the thoughts that are occupying your mind but really just try and focus on your breath.
- After at least 20 inhalations and exhalations read out a positive affirmation, 'I am wealthy'. Continue repeating this affirmation at least 20 times. As you breathe in read the affirmation and on exhalation read it again in your mind.
- If you continue to repeat this positive affirmation every night for 30 days I am positive that you will have programmed your subconscious mind to think positively and gear it towards your money-making goals.

Exercise 2 - Trataka

Sit down on your knees (if you can't do that, sit cross legged). Keep your spine straight. Place a lighted candle on a box at least one to two feet away from eye level. Inhale and exhale slowly and deeply and concentrate your attention on the candle flame. Try not to wink or strain the eyes. After a few seconds or more, your eyes will begin to water. Close them for a second and visualize the flame inside you and believe that you are being energised. You can repeat a positive affirmation such as 'I am confident', 'I am wealthy'. Do this exercise at least 3-4 times a week and I am confident that you will notice significant changes in your lifestyle.

This exercise should be conducted for at least 10 minutes.

Chapter 4

Health And Wealth With Yoga

If your brain waves are unbalanced and you have no control whatsoever of your subconscious mind you will not develop the ability or confidence to make money. Remember the mind comprises of both the conscious and subconscious parts. The conscious mind can be compared to a computer screen, with the subconscious the hard drive.

The conscious mind is the objective reality; it reflects the power of the subconscious. It expresses whatever the subconscious mind stores. Thus it is the logical and rational state of reality. The subconscious is the storehouse of emotions, creativity and your latent powers. Whatever is imprinted on the subconscious mind stays there.

Our senses, such as sight, smell and hearing, pick up impressions of the world around us and store that information in the subconscious mind. It may not be a direct action. Just as the plant, by the method of osmosis, takes in oxygen from the sun's rays through a process of photosynthesis, so too the subconscious mind will absorb whatever is in its environment. Whereas the plant can expel carbon dioxide out into the environment, we as

humans cannot expel anything from the subconscious mind unless we make a certain actionable decision to do so.

Unlike a computer, which is limited by its hard drive capacity to store information, our subconscious mind is an infinite storehouse. There is no end to its limits of storing information. Both the conscious and subconscious mind are not parts of the brain. The brain is a quantifiable organ. It can be seen with the biological eye. It can be dissected and investigated. However, the mind is accessible only through technology related to the spiritual sciences. Whatever is imprinted in the subconscious mind will fuel the conscious mind and you will act out whatever data is stored in your personal hard drive.

According to yoga theory, you have the power to remove data that is harmful, negative, corrupted or illogical. You can replace the data stored in millions of files (the cells) and *nadis* (psychic centres) and the *chakras* (energy centres). I will explain these concepts over the following pages.

Foster the belief in your mind 'I will become a millionaire' - watch how you start to accumulate wealth.

TOP TIP

A Short History ofYoga

Yoga is an ancient tradition stretching back thousands of years. Its birthplace is India. The word yoga itself is derived from the Sanskrit word 'yog' meaning 'to yoke' or bring together. Sanskrit is an ancient classical Indian language. The word yoga also means 'union' of the mind, body and spirit.

It is difficult to date exactly when yoga was born, as traditionally yoga practice was taught to students through word of mouth, with students in turn memorising the teachings. However, evidence that it has been around for many centuries can be gleaned from early ancient Sanskrit texts including the *Vedas* and the *Upanishads*. The *Bhagavad Gita*, dated to around 350BC, also contains references to yoga. However, in the second century BC, Patanjali, a philosopher and teacher of yoga codified this existing oral knowledge about yoga into his classical masterpiece text known as the '*Yoga Sutras*'.

The *Yoga Sutras* explain the eight limbs (steps) of yoga. Patanjali described yoga as the "stilling of the chatterings of the mind." The *Sutras* explain how the mind can be brought under control. When the mind is still, calm and relaxed the body and spirit will also be calm and healthy. Yoga exercises are therefore designed around this concept.

Archaeological excavations in the Indus Valley region (in present day Pakistan) uncovered seals showing deities in yoga postures leading scholars to believe that yoga was being practised by this ancient civilisation in the BC era. Many fitness fashions and sports trends have come and gone over the years. However, yoga has remained intact to this day.

The Significance ofYoga

Yoga is not a sport *per se* it is a lifestyle and ultimately it is concerned with spirituality. An example of this is the practice of meditative techniques to achieve higher states of consciousness and awareness, not only of oneself but also of higher forces. Yoga can be practised by anyone and your goal doesn't necessarily have to be enlightenment (*samadhi*). Yoga can be practised to tone up bums and tums, and to aid weight loss. It can be used to delay the onset of ageing and improve the longevity of the body.

There are over 100 styles of yoga that wannabe yogis and yoginis can practise. It can be quite daunting for a newcomer to know which style is best suited to them and

If your brain waves are unbalanced and you have no control whatsoever on your subconscious mind you will not develop the ability or confidence to make money. **TOP TIP**

their needs. There are a handful of classical styles of yoga including *kundalini* (techniques are designed to awaken the inner serpent or energy known to reside at the base of the spine), *bhakthi* (the yoga of devotional love), *hatha* (physical yoga), *jnana* (yoga philosophy and of the mind), *laya* (working with energy centres the *chakras*). These styles were formulated centuries ago and remain largely unchanged to this day.

During the 18th and 19th Centuries yoga was introduced to the West by such luminaries as Swami Vivekananda. Then in the 1960's yoga enjoyed a resurgence of activity during the flower power era with the help of the Beatles who visited India to study meditation. Since then it has steadily grown to become a mainstream discipline.

Over the centuries (especially the 20th and 21st Centuries) secondary styles of yoga have emerged. The greatest surge of yoga activity has, ironically, been in the West, rather than the East. Yoga practices have been adapted to changing climates, people and conditions. These secondary styles of yoga are sometimes named after the 'teacher' who has taught them.

There are also, what I would classify as, 'hybrid' styles of yoga. These combine the practise of traditional yoga with a contemporary sport or trend. There are exciting variations including yoga-boxing, aquatic yoga, yoga diving, yoga-pilates to name a few.

For the purposes of your goal to make money I recommend you concentrate on the classical styles of yoga and some secondary styles that also offer good exercises based on classical ancient yoga practices.

However, if you want to concentrate purely on the body then one of the hybrid styles may be more suited to you.

Why Practice Yoga?

The ultimate aim of a yoga practice is to achieve *Samadhi*, or enlightenment, a connection with the world around us. This may seem a lofty ideal for many and indeed does require consistent practise and effort to achieve. However, people begin a yoga practice for many different reasons and enlightenment may not actually be their end-goal. Yoga is a holistic therapy for the mind, body and spirit. Anyone can practise yoga. It is the fastest growing health therapy globally, with millions of people practising it. And there is a reason for its massive popularity - it actually works.

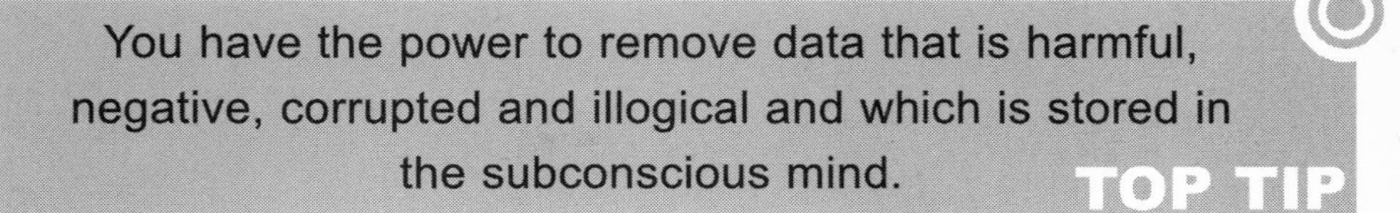

Medical and scientific research shows that yoga can help with hundreds of different ailments including diabetes, cancer, asthma and arthritis with significant results. Regular yoga practise also improves your brainpower, levels of concentration, stamina, sex life and confidence. Yoga practise has been used successfully to delay the symptoms of menopause in women and andropause in men delaying the ageing process to the body.

Today many celebrities practise yoga, including Madonna, Christy Turlington, Cindy Crawford and Uri Geller. They have all contributed to its current popularity. However, the fact that yoga has survived for millennia is evidence of its lasting legacy and credibility as a therapy for truly benefiting the whole body.

A healthy yoga practice will combine different techniques depending on your needs. There are different types of yoga exercises that you can master. These include *asana* (body posture), meditation, *pranayama* (breathing) and mantra (chanting/sacred sound). Yoga is not a religion. However, there are religions in the Indian sub-continents who have their own unique spiritual yoga practises.

You can master yoga whatever level, age or state of health you are in because there will always be exercises which can be tailored or modified to your needs. If you want to get fit and tone your body then you can concentrate solely on the physical postures. If you want to work with the brain and mind then there are meditation practises that you can try. So you see yoga is very accessible.

Channelling Your Energy

Human beings are special and unique creatures. But we must not forget we are also connected to the world. *Prana* is a vital substance and, according to yoga theory, it can be channelled through the body's energy channels known as the *nadis*. These are akin to small energy centres. They are a network of channels running through the body fuelled by *prana*. *Nadis* should not be confused with arteries because yoga does not describe them as such. They are invisible to the naked eye.

Allowing *prana* to move freely through these channels can help to dramatically improve the mind, body and spirit. How is this done? Various yoga exercises can help unblock the negative charges that may have corrupted the *nadis*. For instance, *pranayama* (breathing) techniques can be used to help cleanse, purify and eliminate toxins.

In this context toxins does not necessarily refer only to chemical imbalances or man-made substances, but also

Practising yoga can help you become rich. It also improves brain power, levels of concentration, stamina, confidence and delay the onset of ageing. **TOP TIP**

negative emotions such as hate, anger, fear and jealousy. As human beings we have all experienced such emotions it is what makes us human. However, if any of these emotions is allowed to grow in strength it can cause a major obstruction to well-being and physical health.

Medical and scientific research shows how stress, anxiety and depression, for example, often caused by such emotions, can have serious repercussions on the body. Toxic stress can kill. Such negative emotions in excess can also cause cancer, ulcers and many other diseases that dramatically reduce the quality of life. Thus, they need to be kept under control. Yoga technology offers a blueprint for living. By practising its exercises you can help release these toxins that may be the root cause of the negative static charges that prevent you from moving on successfully in your life.

In addition to the *nadis* there are, according to yoga philosophy, thousands of energy centres in the body known as '*chakras*' meaning wheels. Practitioners have identified seven major *chakras* as being extremely important. Ancient classical texts describe these *chakras* as centres of great energy. They are located through the body and situated at major plexus centres of the physical body.

Chakra	Location
Muladhara the seed chakra also means foundation and is related to the earth. Governs shelter, hunger, thirst, want.	**1st Chakra** - located in the pelvis (base of spine) between the anus and the genitals.
Svadishthana meaning the 'dwelling place'. Its associated element is water. Governs emotional states relating to sexual feelings including jealousy, anger, greed, hate.	**2nd Chakra** - located in the sexual genital area.
Manipura meaning the 'city of gems' and related to fire. Governs the ego and identity.	**3rd Chakra** - located in the navel region.
Anahata meaning the 'unstruck' and related to air. Governs unconditional love, passion and love.	**4th Chakra** - located in the heart.
Vishuddha meaning unadulterated or pure and related to sound. Governs communication.	**5th Chakra** - located in the throat region.
Ajna meaning authority or infinite power. Has no related element but is connected to the planet Saturn. Governs clairvoyance, spirituality and the higher senses.	**6th Chakra** - located near the pineal gland, the 3rd eye point between the eyebrows.
Sahasrara meaning thousand petalled or emptiness. Has no related element but is connected to the planet, Ketu. Governs wisdom, intellect and super intelligence.	**7th Chakra** - located in the cranium (the head).

Yoga technology is a blue-print for living.

TOP TIP

Each *chakra* is responsible for a variety of different things, including our emotional state.

If energy is blocked at any one of these centres then the negative effects will be felt in our life. For instance, the seventh *chakra, sahasrara* is your centre of intelligence, powers of concentration, creativity and wisdom. The fourth *chakra, anahata* relates to unconditional love, our spiritual and literal love, passion and desire. The second *chakra, Svadishthana* is your sexual centre, as well as your centre for creativity, It's associated with reproduction and all bodily fluids. Sanskrit is a complex and fascinating language. For each word there are several meanings. I have provided a synopsis of the seven major *chakras* in the body in the table on the previous page, together with their associated basic meanings and other information.

If prana is channelled effectively through the chakras it can dramatically escalate the removal of the toxins and fuel these energy centres so that they are working efficiently and maximum benefits are experienced. Our hair, our skin renews itself.

We are in a perpetual cycle of rebirth as is the universe. Yoga is one discipline where exercises are designed to improve the quality of energy your energy. Learn to tap into this powerful force. The universe is made of energy. We are energy; our cells are molecules of energy. The whole earth is energy!

Ancient belief systems may hold the key too many of man's perplexities regarding the meaning of life and the workings of our mind, body and spirit. For example, the ancient Chinese classical text, *I Ching* contains cryptic mathematical codes which could be one of the earliest texts describing the concept that we know today as DNA. What are the origins of man, and what are the building blocks that create the foundation of life itself? There are many explanations given by different religious and spiritual traditions.

Science is making some headway in explaining this vexed question, but it has a long way to go to conclusively prove our make-up, however, one of the greatest developments of the last century was the discovery of the genetic code.

The model of this, which you may have seen, is a double helix and the information stored inside the DNA (deoxyribonucleic acid molecules). Just by taking a swab of someone's blood you can investigate their DNA and link them to scenes of crime or explore their genetic make-up, such as their disposition to certain disease and other factors. Having this information is a powerful weapon. It

By practising yoga you can release toxins that are the root of the negative static charge which is preventing you from making money. **TOP TIP**

allows us to make comparisons with fossilized humans' centuries old and establish our similarities or differences. It also allows us to refute past historical and scientific paradigms.

Unlocking Your Unique Code

Genes and the DNA they contain are fascinating aspects of our bodies. Everything on a molecular level contains similar building blocks that make up life itself. This is a great stride for human kind. This means that animals too contain DNA with their own blueprint and genetic make-up. It also means that now medical and scientific researchers can directly manipulate the very fabric of life itself raising questions of ethics, such as the cloning of animals. It also poses questions as to whether humans too will be cloned in the near future.

The discovery of genes and DNA allows research to be conducted which can be of startling benefit to mankind, for example breaking the codes of parasites that can cause disease allowing for the formulation of vaccines. This knowledge allows access to a completely new methodology for mapping the future. The human body requires different types of protein to function. Contained within each of our cells is the DNA which acts as a 'scientist' sending out 'orders' to the body to create proteins.

Our genes build each one of us. Genes are a blueprint of our life. They contain vast stores of information and technology. As human beings we can directly inherit certain characteristics and traits from our parents and their lineage. By tracing the genetic makeup of the body scientists can manipulate DNA and create many different things.

There are trillions of cells in the body yet each one of them has a DNA code. Inside the DNA are letters. These letters are the code that determines who we are. Within the DNA strands we find the genes and each gene is further comprised of the chromosomes. If it is possible ever to read and understand each of these unique codes and read the stores of information housed there mankind will have entered a super-era of knowledge. Yoga theory has always accepted that the body is a storehouse of information and it's not all stored in the brain (the traditional Western orthodox medical and scientific view). In fact, data is carried all around the body.

DNA can be continuously duplicated and always it will create the four essential molecules of the same type known as nucleotides. A DNA molecule looks like a spiral shape of

Learn to work with the energy field that surrounds you.

TOP TIP

two strands. When a new cell is born the DNA replicates itself (RNA) into one strand. Essentially it is the same but is of a different shape. According to yoga theory we also inherit traits from our previous lives or generations or parents (there are many different terms you can apply here).

Science tells us that this hereditary information is passed on in the chromosomes which are imprinted into the chemical pattern of DNA. So, for example, the colour of your hair and your physical make-up, as well as disease can be passed down to you by inheriting this genetic make-up from your parents.

Genes can be replicated by the body and information transmitted. Indeed human are not unique because all molecular creatures on the planet contain similar basic DNA. Although RNA is a copy of the DNA, further scientific research is needed to establish whether RNA once copied remains a blueprint of the DNA or whether it then creates its own data and thereby a new structure.

Ancient yoga theory speaks of the *nadis*, carriers of *prana* and essentially life itself. However, they are also carriers of the mind. Should scientists also be looking closely at the yoga theory of *nadis*?

Reprogramming Your Mind for Riches

According to yoga theory, the brain stores information in the form of energy, but also in the millions of nadis. Data is transferred throughout the mind body and spirit. If you want to be rich then you need to manipulate the data that is passing through this trinity. This is possible, but it requires a direct and conscious reprogramming of your mind.

By using yoga exercise and believing in your entitlement and worth to become rich, you will indeed become wealthy. Do not dismiss your body as just something you live in because inside there is a complex and amazing system of data transferral that makes up who you are and determines your life expectancy, however it also dictates the way you act and react to the world around you.

The brain contains millions of nerve cells, within each of which are energy-producing bodies called mitochondria. The mitochondria influence our metabolism by producing small electrical currents. These electrical currents can be directed into different wave frequencies in the brain, and each of them is responsible for specific experiences.

> Meditation and related practices not only still the mind but also help to unleash your creative potential.
>
> **TOP TIP**

These are generally classified into the following types:

- Alpha
- Beta
- Theta
- Delta
- SMR

These electrical currents operate through the synapses, specialized junctions which are the body's telephone exchange, through which the cells of the nervous system signal to one another and to non-neneuronal cells such as those in muscles or glands.

Synapses form the circuits in which the neurons of the central nervous system interconnect. They are thus crucial to the biological computations that underlie perception and thought. They also provide the means through which the nervous system connects to and controls the other systems of the body. The synapses, which are located in the nerve cells, are key players and responsible for a number of our activities including behaviour, physical and psychological health, as well as memory and sleep patterns.

If our energy frequencies are unbalanced, then the brain is negatively affected. It is a bit like putting in the wrong oil and phobias can be alleviated or controlled.

into a car engine. Conversely, when the energy frequencies in the brain are stabilised and balanced, then chronic conditions such as anxiety, depression, lack of concentration, complexes and phobias can be alleviated or controlled.

In yoga meditation, techniques are designed to balance these frequencies so that the mind-body-spirit continuum works in harmony, helping you to improve your IQ, develop your talents and access a higher state of being. Remember that if any of the brainwaves are unbalanced, the communication network between the brain and the central nervous system will be disrupted, causing you long-term psychological and physical problems.

Releasing Negative Energy for Wealth

If you release that store of negativity from the subconscious mind I am certain that you will change the way you live. Our body is a mass of energy. The universe is a mass of energy. We are a microcosm of the world. We are a reflection of the natural world. Inside us are trillions of cells, each with a life force of its own. Each cell is a tiny world. According to yoga our mind permeates our whole existence it permeates each cell of our body.

We are not just one person we are many personas. Each day we die our cells are in a continual process of renewal.

Money is a powerful weapon - use it wisely

TOP TIP

Over the years we are continually dying and being reborn.

Our organs are never static they are continuously being powered by *prana* a life force energy that is invisible to the human eye. Classical yoga texts describe it as the force that keeps us alive. The ancient Indians were remarkable in identifying this force. The ancient Chinese too speak of a life force energy known as 'chi'.

Traditional Indian and Chinese medicine base diagnosis on the flow of energy through the body. If our energy is negative it can stagnate in the mind, the body and the spirit. The spirit is a term used in this context loosely to define our consciousness, our mind, our sixth sense, our ability as humans to reach beyond the body and out of it, and our connection to the world, the universe and beyond.

Science now accepts that there are limits to its capacity to explain everything about the world in which we live. However, great strides are being made to investigate the supernatural and super-conscious realms of existence. We still have a long way to go. Perhaps we will never have the super-intelligence to completely explain the workings of our mind and the world. We can turn to the ancient sciences for answers to decipher the meaning of the world and look within its hidden codes and messages for clues about who we are and why we act the way we do.

The files in the subconscious mind are highly advanced; it is a sophisticated system of storage. You will recall that one set of files stored there relates specifically to money (how you deal with it, perceive it, and so forth). If there is a static charge on this file, it may be preventing you from creating wealth.

Maybe you grew up in a household where you were taught money was the root of all evil. Or perhaps you were put down and people said you would never be rich. These negative statements become deep-rooted in your psychology and you will react to the world around you in similar fashion. If this is the case, try to think not of money itself as the evil, but as you would a knife. It is not intrinsically bad what the item is used for is the critical factor.

Here are a few exercises to help you deal with your negativity (if you have any). They have been taken from Zen (Japanese yoga) traditions to help improve your prospects of making money. Zen yoga has its roots in Indian yoga. They are from the same family. The exercises may look deceptively simple, but as you learn to master them you will note they require some effort. Once you have

Money is energy learn to tap into this 'energy'.

TOP TIP

mastered them, you will definitely experience noticeable changes in your psychology and body.

Remember, they are derived from yoga and were not necessarily designed for making money per se. The irony is as you regularly practise yoga your creativity improves and your mind-power is boosted. You can use this mind power to 'make money'.

Exercise 1: Watch Your Step

Wake up early in the morning. Take a few long deep breaths. Go to the park or out into the garden or at the least somewhere where there is grass. Failing this, any place where you can take at least 50 steps.

While you are standing, put your arms at your sides. Drop your head down and stare at your right foot. Gaze at it for a second or two; then while you are still staring at it lift it up and move forward bringing it down to the floor. Now shift your attention to your left foot, lift it and walk forward one step. Repeat with your right leg and then your left.

Repeat again.

Take small steps.

When you are watching the steps, tell yourself you will watch your step when making money and that you will save it. Take at least 50 steps.

After a few weeks of daily or weekly practice, you will notice a change in how you handle your money matters and other affairs because your concentration levels will hopefully improve.

Originally, this exercise was used in ancient times to improve concentration and for higher meditative purposes. It was used by the great lamas in Tibet, by followers of Zen in Thailand and Indian Tantrika yogis.

Exercise 2: Harness Your Thoughts

Sit down in any pose (lotus, cross-legged or on your knees).

Let the mind roam free. Let whatever thoughts are occupying it move around them.

Now try to visualise the thoughts. Imagine you are actually looking at them swirling around inside your head.

Watch them for five minutes. As you master the exercise you can increase the time to six or even seven minutes.

Don't stop visualising the thoughts. Allow the breath to come up from the stomach and then close your eyes.

Let your belly go in and out slowly and focus in on the navel at the centre. Stop the thoughts floating. This is a difficult exercise to master, but once you have grasped it you will be surprised at its great benefits.

The breath should come from the navel centre (your belly button). Shift your attention to this centre. In between, if your mind starts wandering, harness the thoughts and keep diverting your attention back to the navel centre. You will find that your heart may beat faster and you will breathe more quickly. This exercise will help you access the deep state faster. So you don't have to waste time 'trying to sleep'. This will also help you remain grounded and calm, thereby helping you produce better-quality work and stop you from being lazy and slobbing out in sleep for more hours than you need.

If your mind keeps wandering, keep bringing it back to the navel. Don't restrain your breath; breathe normally (not long or slow). This exercise should be performed for at least half an hour.

Long-term practitioners of Zen and yoga can sit for hours practising this one exercise. You will notice in a few weeks or months that your whole personality will change for the better.

Your physical body will change too as it becomes more attuned with the calmness of the mind your posture improves, helping you walk better and exude confidence.

This exercise also helps to reduce anxiety and depression as it helps the glucose in the blood to flow at a more normal rate. If you do not have serious diabetes, this exercise will benefit you. Also, your brain releases stress and you will feel better.

Exercise 3: Night Reflection

When you are about to go to sleep (at least 45 minutes beforehand), learn to monitor and observe the activities you have participated in or seen that day. Start from the minute when you are sitting, standing or lying down and work backwards.

Maybe you were brushing your teeth before you lay down. Did you use particular toothpaste? Where were you? Attempt to remember everything you can in minute detail, including colours, shapes and even what may appear to be insignificant things.

Keep recalling your activities for as long as possible. At least start with the five minutes immediately preceding from where you are standing, lying or sitting. You may find it difficult to keep going back at first, but keep going. In this way, you can keep increasing the time of recollection. There will come a time when you will be able to monitor your half-day or even the full day.

If you don't like an event, person or something that happened during the day you can mentally confront the events or activities you dislike.

Some incidents can trigger past bad memories. When you continually and habitually scan the day's events, you can increasingly take charge of your emotions. You will become happier and more confident all good qualities to have when you set about making money. However, erasing negative habits and emotions to help you access the file of prosperity does not come quickly.

You need to work on programming the subconscious mind regularly. There is no real long-term success to be gained by simply working the exercises for a few weeks and then abandoning them. It must be long-term for sustainable success. You must constantly practice the exercises a few times a month, not a few times a year, to gain maximum benefit. As mentioned above the money file can be accessed. There are certain techniques, if practised regularly that can help you release the static charge. They include asanas (physical postures), mantras (sacred sound) and meditation.

The Emotional Key to Wealth

Now here's the buzz. The emotions, which relate to wealth, are stored in the mind. Once you release any negative attachments you associate with your long-term wealth status, you will be freer and more confident about making money. You will also develop your sixth sense, learn to trust your gut instincts to spot money making ideas, and have the courage and determination to pursue your aims and ambitions. Do not let your bad habits prevent you from achieving your maximum potential? Research shows that regular performance of meditation increases your levels of intelligence and stamina.

Your subconscious houses millions of files. These have grown since childhood and contain vast stores of data about your life and experiences. So if you were brought up in a household that loathed money and believed that rich people were evil, those memories are stored there. Or if you were bullied, those memories are stored here. Your emotions, and how you react to the world as an adult, are the result and by-product of how you coped with childhood events and incidents.

An unhealthy mind will prevent you from achieving your goals. However, you can positively exercise the mind with meditation and yoga breathing exercises (*pranayama*). You can't work and achieve great feats if your mind is cluttered with negative emotions and bad habits.

When you learn to channel positive energy, this helps to improve your skills and talents. And when you are on the road to making riches, there are certain skills you need in abundance, including patience and the ability to learn to deal with stress.

Practice of *pranayama* should be an integral part of any yogic practice and lifestyle. *Pranayama* exercises range from simple to extremely complicated. If you incorporate any type of *pranayama* exercise into your daily routine you will experience noticeable and beneficial effects to your whole well-being.

Always remember the three basic components of *pranayama*. These are *puraka* (inhalation), *rechaka* (exhalation) and *kumbhaka* (retention of breath). The definitions given for these acts are simplistic ones, but they should at least give you an idea of the workings of the breath. Ancient yogis and some of today's practitioners, use *pranayama* as a tool to access higher spiritual states and for tapping into the subconscious mind.

When *pranayama* exercises are taught you may come across terms such as 'sets' or 'rounds' these refer to the number of times you should perform the *purakas, rechakas* or *kumbhakas.* Just as musical compositions have their own notes, so too *pranayama* exercises have their own compositions.

If *pranayama* is practised incorrectly it can have a negative effect on your mind and body. Therefore it is imperative that you follow any instructions given to you whether in this book, on a DVD, in a yoga class or elsewhere, properly. Always remember the goal or objective of your *pranayama* practice. What is it? What should it be? Ultimately it should be to control the breath and then the mind. *Pranayama* helps to still the mind and bring inner peace. That is the essence of yoga. And, as your practice improves and becomes regular you will soon begin to enjoy it too.

Pranayama practice has consequences aside from the ultimate goal. Off shoots of practising *pranayama* regularly include help in losing weight, aiding concentration, relieving stress and reducing anxiety to name a few. When these positive results begin to impact the mind and body you will feel much healthier, happier and more in control of your life. You will enjoy good health - essential if you want to become rich.

I would highly recommend you incorporate the following yoga exercises into your yoga practice - *Anulom Vilom Pranayama* and *Kapal Bhathi*. I believe that only after 14 days you will experience significant changes to your mind, and you will feel healthier and energized. Don't take my word for it - try them yourselves. Remember these exercises have been around for thousands of years - if they have been around that long and are still being taught and practised today what does that say about yoga? It has a credible lineage and legacy.

Kapal Bhathi

If you perform this exercise regularly you will notice many benefits. This is a breathing and cleansing exercise that strengthens the immune system. It also helps to reduce fat in the stomach and dramatically strengthens the respiratory system and the organs. It is an excellent 'pick-me-up' exercise and it refreshes the nerves.

Your sense of sight, smell and sound markedly improve after a few weeks of regular performance and you will feel lighter, fresher and enjoy a restful sleep. The lungs, rib cage and the heart all benefit from this exercise. The general lustre of the skin also improves, and your mind will feel stable and calmer improving your powers of concentration, creativity and stamina. The essence of the *kapal bhahti* is the movements of the breath through the nose and stomach. It is a cleansing breath that dramatically improves your physical health and cleanses both the *chakras* and the *nadis*.

How to perform:-

- Sit down either on your knees or cross-legged. Keeping your spine straight and upright, place your hands onto knees and touch your thumbs to your index fingers.
- Close your eyes and mouth, and concentrate on the third eye point (situated between the eyebrows).
- Exhale quickly, swiftly and forcefully. The exhalation should come from the navel region. When exhaling your navel should be pushed back causing you to automatically inhale.

The exhalation of breath should be in a second, and with practice gradually increase the momentum to two to three exhalations per second.

Continue this exercise for at least 15-20 minutes.

At the end, hold the breath; pull navel in and back, squeezing your sexual organs. When you feel uncomfortable, exhale breath out completely and push navel in and back again. Hold this position for a few seconds with your eyes closed. Your inner energy will rise.

Anulom Vilom Pranayama

This is a wonderful exercise that will help clean your subconscious mind and release negativity, thereby helping you to overcome obstacles in your life. This exercise is also recommended for people suffering from a range of conditions including restlessness, nervousness, migraines, headaches, tension and hypertension, and heart problems.

How to perform:-

Sit down comfortably in easy pose (cross-legged) or lotus posture (right leg on left thigh and left leg on right thigh).

- Close and hold the right nostril with thumb.
- Inhale deeply through the left nostril.
- When you complete the inhalation, place middle andring fingers on your left nostril to close it. Take the thumb off the right nostril and exhale.

- When the exhalation is completed, inhale immediately from the same, i.e. the right, nostril. On completion of the inhalation, place thumb again on the right nostril and close it.

- Now lift off your middle and ring fingers from your left nostril and exhale. On completion of the exhalation immediately inhale from the same nostril, i.e. the left, nostril. Continue following this same pattern.

Continue this exercise for at least 15 minutes.

The exercises

Perform the yoga exercises listed on the previous pages first thing in the morning. All the major religious and spiritual traditions have specific practices for the morning. For instance, Muslims have *tahajjid* and *fajir*. Whilst Sikhs practise *amrit vela*. Morning is a significant time for recharging and cleansing yourself spiritually. If you start the day in this way you will feel calm and grounded during the day.

I have covered some yoga exercises in this book. Try some and I guarantee you will begin to appreciate not only your own inner power, but also learn to tune in to the environment around you. The ancient Indian yogis did not design exercises to access material gains, but there is no doubt that they can be used to improve the way you access money. This may appear to be unethical, but when you make money you then have the option of sharing it with people who deserve it. Imagine how good you would feel if you had extra cash to donate to worthwhile community and charitable projects!

My dear father used to say: "Share and you will receive in abundance." There is an unwritten law of the universe contributing and helping in charitable projects will make you feel happier. Tap into the wealth file in your brain using yoga and make money. Today, millions of people around the world are discovering this ancient discipline for themselves.

In the UK, yoga-related workshops, classes and seminars have successfully been introduced into the NHS, into schools, onto the national curriculum, into prisons and many other places where relaxation as well as revitalization is needed. Yoga's supporters are legendary. Cleopatra, the famed queen of ancient Egypt, practised yoga. Marilyn Monroe, icon of the silver screen, incorporated yoga into her fitness regime. The father of Western psychology, CG Jung, practised yoga and wrote about it extensively.

Jung's seminar on *Kundalini* yoga, presented to the Psychological Club in Zurich in 1932, is regarded as a milestone in the psychological understanding of Eastern thought, and of the symbolic transformations of inner experience. *Kundalini* yoga presented Jung with a model for the developmental phases of higher consciousness, and he interpreted its symbols in terms of the process of individuation.

There is increasing research into the benefits of practicing yoga combined with credible findings that it really does help to improve tone and contour your body perfectly. It has also been used to defy ageing, boost energy levels, relieve stress and anxiety, build up stamina and confidence. and gently work on the spirit to help you feel happier and more alive.

Yoga is an excellent therapy that everyone should try. Yoga is a technology - it is unique. There are different types of exercises including meditation that can dramatically change your health, for the better. Research shows that regular practise of yoga can help with many conditions. The body of evidence supporting these claims continue to increase. Yoga offers a unique set of procedures that can be accessed by anyone, to help manage crisis situations and overload.

If you incorporate yoga into your lifestyle and practise it consistently I am sure that you too will feel the positive impact in your life. Yoga can make you rich. This may appear to be a startling conclusion for some. It may even appear to be unethical by others. Let's not forget that yoga is in essence a spiritual practice. However, yoga practices per se can dramatically improve your 'energy' levels and release negativity, including the static charge that rests in the subconscious mind, which may have prevented you in becoming successful and wealthy in your life so far.

Harnessing the Power of the Mind

There is a technique that has been used for centuries throughout the world to help boost the power of the brain.

It is a powerful methodology that many spiritual and religious disciplines have used for a variety of purposes. Over the last few years countless studies have been conducted, both scientific and sociological, to help establish the benefits of this ancient force. What is it?

And how can it help you? This methodology is popularly known in the West as 'meditation'. In the East meditation remains a practice that is deeply embedded in the fabric of everyday life for many people.

Scientists are now paying close attention to practitioners and the effects meditation has on their psychology and biology. There are different types of meditation practices taught in different parts of the world.

Practice of Meditation:

- Reduces stress and anxiety. It improves confidence, Stamina and builds up the immune system.
- Helps improve brainpower, including memory.
- Improves creativity and concentration skills.
- Helps to manage many ailments including depression And addictions.

Meditation and related practices not only still the mind, but also help to unleash your creative potential. It's scientifically proven that practising meditation can significantly improve your mind power. Remember the whole purpose of yoga is to still the mind. If the mind is calm, then the body is too. Calmer minds produce greater creativity and ideas. There are different techniques you can use to help the mind settle. If you master the following exercises, you can tap into your deeper subconscious mind and into your infinite powers.

You can make money releasing the static charge in your subconscious mind. Whatever you listen to, see, hear and touch (i.e. any information that reaches the mind from the senses) is all recorded within us. You may be surprised to learn that so much information is actually stored there. You may think you have forgotten what happened. But you will be surprised, given the right conditions, how much of the day and its events you could potentially remember.

When you leave the house in the morning you are exposed to a whole array of external stimuli. From the hundreds if not thousands of people you encounter to the colours you see, sounds you hear and the smells that assault your senses. But you don't consciously remember everything. According to yoga theory however, the data is all recorded within you, in the subconscious mind. Just as a plant takes in the energy of the light through photosynthesis, so too the human body absorbs its environment.

All spiritual traditions recommend the practise of sacred sound and meditation, especially in the early morning. All major religions encompass this concept. This is a great time to charge your energy levels. There is a wonderful saying that I enjoy: "Early to bed, early to rise makes a man (or woman)healthy, wealthy and wise."

Money is a form of 'energy and I recently put this statement to Dr David Pearl, a world authority on the subject of energy. He agreed that money is indeed energy. In a recent meeting with him he told me when his 'teachers' are imparting their method of healing they always charge some money, a form of consideration. Giving and receiving is loaded with energy.

To make money you have to train the subconscious mind to accept that you will receive it and not only have the talent and skills needed to become rich, but that wanting money is not an evil wish. Some people are embarrassed to ask for money, others shy away from the subject. This is a direct result of one's conditioning. If you grew up in a household believing that money brought nothing but misery and untold evil then those negative attitudes will have imprinted themselves into your subconscious mind.

However, if you were brought up in a wealthy household your perception of money will typically may be very different money is a powerful weapon and many who are wealthy will agree. Indeed, all the millionaires I have spoken to agree that money definitely raises the quality of one's lifestyle.

Chapter 5

Getting Out Of Prison Mode

THE TIME FOR BEING PASSIVE IS OVER. Now that you've set your objectives, developed and followed your plan, and realised the importance of believing in yourself, it would be nice to know what tools are available for economic prosperity. As the foundation for becoming a millionaire has been laid, it is now time to learn how you can make it work for you 24 hours a day, 7 days a week.

You should always save, save, save. Save for a 'rainy day' - don't assume that the people who you think you can rely on now will be there to help when things go bad for you. How much you have to save varies depending upon how long you want to wait to become a millionaire.

Interest is something with which we are all familiar from the relatively low rates of student loans from the college days of yesteryear, to the astronomical interest rates on credit cards after the amazingly short grace period has expired. The rate of interest charged by both individuals and institutions when they loan money in any of its numerous forms (i.e. bonds, credit, commercial loans, or mortgages) is the price you pay as the borrower for the use of someone else's money. This is obviously of benefit to the lender, who is going to receive more than he or she loaned from both the principal and the interest paid.

In the world of banks, this can work to your advantage on the route to becoming a millionaire. Essentially, banks are in the business of lending money. In the United States, which has one of the largest economies in the world, the rate of interest banks charge depends on the short-term interest rate set by the Federal Reserve Board.

Interest rates drive various savings accounts and Certificates of Deposit (CDs), since banks will adjust the interest charged on loans to make sure of profits. In turn, this will affect the likelihood that consumers will seek loans for mortgages, entrepreneur ventures, and all manner of other investments, all of which are important indicators of the strength of a nation's economy. Why is this relevant to you? Because the combination of interest and compounding will turn your savings into a million dollars or it could completely bankrupt you and destroy your investments.

Obviously, the less money you invest, the longer it is going to take. Investments comprise a whole range of things including shares, property and businesses.

Keep on top of current financial affairs as well as a keen eye on the markets, latest trends and new ideas.

TOP TIP

For many people compound interest is the secret to the phenomenon of rapid wealth growth, and you need not do the calculations yourself. There are several software programs and charts available in stores, over the Internet, or in your local library that will assist you. A good reputable financial adviser can also help you understand this principle and how you can make it work for you.

What you want to determine is the length of time that it will take you to amass a million dollars. The moral is this: when you save, invest in something with a good annual return. No matter what your annual take-home pay may be, there are surely things that you can forego in order to begin building up your millionaire fund. Remember to stay focused. You need a plan of action detailing, even if it is briefly, how you intend to achieve your aim of making a million. Also keep a note of how much money you wish to accumulate in say one year's time. This will give you something tangible to work towards.

This will not be an overnight process as you have had many years to acquire the bad habit of spending without saving. Additionally, there are factors such as your age and expenses to consider in your attempt to save money.

Nevertheless, any time is a great time to get into the habit of saving and investing. Simply begin by making an honest and determined commitment to set aside a certain percentage of your funds every pay period, in order to realise your dream of becoming a millionaire.

This also means freeing up more of your money by taking steps to reduce the amount of money you pay out on a daily basis. This can take a number of forms, such as doubling the minimum payment on your credit card to avoid the criminally high interest rates that can accrue. Likewise, in every area of your life, you can save money by simply being a smart shopper and avoiding paying more for items than you have to.

Now, what you invest your savings in is crucial. While there are many types of ventures into which you can place your money, one of the more popular is investing in common stocks. With a high rate of return on average, such investments are more likely to make you a millionaire relatively quickly. However, this is not for the risk-averse mindset. Also get good financial advice before you decide to part with your well-earned fortune. Many a company has gone bust, with investors losing their savings.

The offering of stock by a company takes the ownership of a company out of the hands of a few people and offers ownership to the public at large. Those who purchase stock in the company, the stockholders, are the de jure owners of the company, and have power in voting based upon the number of shares they own.

The key to success in the stock market is a relatively simple one: you buy shares when they are at a low price, hoping that the company will perform well over the years, which will raise the stock price, and thus increase your rate of return on the investment when you sell at the higher price. Even if you do not sell, you will own shares in a lucrative company which pays dividends and represents additional income that you can reinvest.

You are advised to consult a specialised and reputable financial broker before jumping in at the deep end and buying investment products. Such brokers are experts in their field of work and understand how the financial markets work and how they can potentially work for you. One thing to keep in mind, however, is the fact that stocks both rise and fall, even the so-called blue-chip stocks, which are the shares of companies with a long and sustained history of growth and prosperity. In order to prevent exposing yourself to the risk of the performance of one company, the solution may be diversification.

Diversification can entail investing in stocks as well as bonds, government treasury bills, or certificates of deposit. However, since the focus in this section is on stock, the vehicle through which you may diversify your investments is mutual funds. A mutual fund is an amalgam of stocks of several different companies.

This spreads out the risk you incur in investing ensuring that not all of your eggs are in one basket, so to speak. While some of the companies in the mutual funds may not be performing up to par, you will not be at a complete loss because the others will be performing satisfactorily. The return on mutual funds varies, as there are several thousands of such funds in the market today. However, many have returns which are well over the 10% mentioned in the previous section. This is an extremely attractive avenue of investment to a professional management company.

The opportunity to allow your money to work for you is at your disposal and the sooner you get started, the better. Do not limit your ambitions or dreams. You only have one shot at this life so aim high. When you want to make money you need to tell yourself over and over 'I can do it' - half-hearted wishes are not enough.

Millionaires accept calculated risks and responsibilities - making money is not for cowards or thieves.

TOP TIP

A few factors may adversely affect your funds as you embark upon this journey. The first is the various kinds of risk associated with dealing in the money markets. A major company in which you have invested may come under poor management and go bankrupt. The Federal Reserve Board or Bank of England may make an interest rate decision that works to your disadvantage. Inflation may soar taking a large bite out of your potential earnings.

The risks are numerous, but nothing comes without risk. It is a part of life, and you should not be discouraged by what could conceivably reduce earnings in the grand scheme of the universe. The fact that tomorrow you may have an untimely meeting with a runaway Mack truck does not mean that you take up the life of an agoraphobic and refrain from leaving your home. In the same manner, risk in the stock market requires you to analyze and appreciate, but should not deter you from investing.

Also, consider taxes and the effect they can have on your earnings. Although you may not live in a socialist country where taxes provide those mutual benefits that the country deems essential, once you begin to increase your wealth, you must give the government its share.

To find out the most effective ways to reduce your tax obligation, it is advisable that you see a financial consultant who will be able to assist you. However, being a millionaire will surely assuage the pain associated with handing a few dollars or pounds over to the government to address society's needs.

Anyone with sincere desire and discipline can become a millionaire. The speed with which this dream is realised depends, inter alia, upon the amount of sacrifice you are willing to make in the short term in order to be prosperous in the long term. You should begin by ensuring that the means of acquiring your income is something about which you feel strongly and thoroughly enjoy.

Life is what we make it, and life as a millionaire will afford one the ability to enjoy life to the fullest. This is not to imply that those without a net worth of a million dollars cannot enjoy life, but simply that most people would prefer the opportunity to spend more time with family and friends. Additionally, not living from pay cheque to pay cheque and not constantly worrying about making ends meet would be a welcome change of circumstances for many.

Don't put all your eggs into one basket.

TOP TIP

Now is the time for you to take the most important step of your life and trust, know, and believe that you can and will achieve. Successful wealth-builders also invest wisely; they don't hold all their wealth in cash-type funds that are easily and readily available on call. They invest in financial products, which cannot be accessed on demand. This helps to maintain discipline in financial spending. Individuals who are unable to increase wealth tend to have their money tied up in material goods that have no appreciative value, for instance cars, watches, clothes, TVs and so forth.

If you feel overwhelmed by the pressures of family spending, isn't it time you cut down on some of your expenses and outgoings? It may be difficult to do at the beginning but if you don't start now, you will find it much more difficult later.

When you budget for yourself (i.e. work out your outgoings), then make it a wider picture and include your family. Help them account for their outgoings. You see, even if you have the millionaire mindset, this is only half the story. If your partner or siblings don't share the same aspirations, it will take you much longer to realise your goal of making a million. High consumption families may spend a significant amount on material goods. Change your and your family's lifestyles. There's no harm in buying the occasional treats, but just don't overdo it.

Do you need aims to make a million? It certainly helps to have aims. When you can establish these in your head and write them down on paper, at least you can begin to work towards them. You can have any number of aims including hoping to become financially independent, not working for anyone for the rest of your life. Financial independence brings with it clearer aims and long-term future success.

Many millionaires spend a lot of time actually planning for their future. You don't need an accounting degree to know that planning effectively will help you realise and save more of your money.

Let's give you a simple example. You want to buy a carton of orange juice. There are lots of shops to choose from. There may already be a few major outlets in your area. When you don't plan, you could end up buying a carton of juice from the nearest convenience store because it's the closest shop to your house. By doing some investigative work, you might find that the same carton you purchased for 68p in the convenience store sells for 38p at another high-street store. It may be a different brand but remains cheaper. If you had purchased in bulk you might even have saved more money.

"*Maya Ko Milay, Maya Kar Kar Lambay Hath*"
Money makes money. Money attracts money
(Tulsi Das - Ancient Indian poet and philosopher)
TOP TIP

But there is no point to buying in bulk if you are going to waste it. Remember, though, that you don't want to spend too much time on finding that cheap carton of orange juice. People who have high-consumption lifestyles always spend a lot more money than those who actually plan how they spend. Wealthy people will spend more time speaking to financial advisors and look for ways to save and invest, even though they are reasonably financially comfortable. People who don't have much wealth are usually spenders.

They continually stress about how they can afford to purchase material goods to live and feed their high consumption lifestyles, keep up with fashion trends and buy the latest gizmos. That's why they never really accumulate wealth, despite having earnings in the high-income bracket.

But there are people who have the mindset and are not spenders per se, but have lots of responsibilities to meet, such as a family. This should not discourage them because in the long run they will have the ability to not only continue to meet their obligations but also make additional money. You can't make money on your own, only other people can make money for you. Your staff, for instance can 'make' or 'break' your businesses.

Chapter 6

Work For Yourself

One of the best ways of making money is to work for yourself (i.e. own your own business or even go into partnership with someone who has a like-minded millionaire mind-set like yourself). A significant number of self-made millionaires became millionaires by working for themselves. But eventually along the road of making a million pounds/dollars you will definitely need other people to help you make a million, whether it's staff, customers, accountants, financial advisors and so forth.

To start making money you have to scrimp and save. Once you have made a fortune you can spend some of it treating yourself and others, but you must remember the golden rule - continue to build your wealth, otherwise you will be left with nothing.

Next time you are shopping in a small corner shop or off-licence on a busy high street, and the man or woman behind the counter looks rough and tired, just remember he or she (if they are the owner) has probably accumulated more wealth in a few years than you as an employee may do in your lifetime.

Another misconception: just because you're in a particular type of business is not evidence that you are a millionaire or wealthy. What does being rich mean to you? Do you think it means having lots and lots of expensive toys and material goods? Do you think that the rich own yachts? Drive expensive cars? Wear expensive clothes? Live in gigantic mansions? Actually, not really.

Although rich people often do own such goods, owning goods does not mean having money in the bank. More often, money accumulates through a strong work ethic and financial discipline. The idea that rich people own many material goods is one spread by the films and TV that we see, and especially by advertising. Next time you see someone dressed head to toe in expensive designer clothes, ask yourself, 'What are they really worth?'

Try and live below your means especially if you want to become a millionaire. For instance if you earn £30,000 pretend to yourself that you only earn £25,000 and you can budget accordingly. The £5,000 can be invested in savings.

The type of business may be a key factor in someone's ability to make money but even more importantly is the owner's character or personality traits. These can determine whether he or she will become a millionaire.

For instance, take two identical businesses, one belonging to Mr. Smith and the other to Mr. Jones. Both businesses generate similar profit margins. Neither

Investigate how many incomes come into your household. Combine incomes to generate wealth quickly.

TOP TIP

Mr. Smith nor Mr. Jones has any other business ventures. Both have families comprising a wife and two children. Yet Mr. Smith is a millionaire and Mr. Jones is not. Why is that? To answer this question you need to explore their lifestyle differences.

While Mr. Smith and his family have what they need in life, they are circumspect, if not downright strict, about unnecessary spending. They lead quiet, unobtrusive lives centred around the family, and are known as good neighbours. Because they put spiritual values ahead of appearances, they do not brag about what they own.

Mr. Smith and his wife share the use of an ordinary estate car, and their children cycle to their respective state schools. They are known for paying their bills on time, and for fair play on and off the sports field. In fact, only their many benefactors, along with the Inland Revenue, really know how generous Mr. Smith can be.

In contrast to that, Mr. Jones drives a sporty Mercedes, and is known for extravagant trips and partying with groups of fellow businessmen. His wife runs a four-wheel-drive Toyota, and flies to her family home in Pakistan a lot for company. Like her, Mr. Jones' children seem to make up for the lack of a satisfactory family life by being extravagant consumers of material goods, and buying attention wherever they go.

Both children are miles behind Mr. Smith's children in academic ability, probably because they place little value on achieving real independence. In fact, they had better start studying fast because a recession is just around the corner, and Mr. Jones' business is in danger of collapsing because he has not saved adequately against that rainy day. So, just because you are self-employed doesn't mean you are a millionaire.

Many self-employed people also struggle financially, sometimes for many years. But the point is, when you are self-employed, the likelihood of your making money is far higher than it is for someone who is not.

Another point to remember, millionaires don't tend to own just one business. They may have several. When these are combined together, they generate the wealth that puts them in the millionaire category (although there are some rare cases that did). Also, surprisingly, they may be making money in industries and businesses that people tend to think as unconventional or not very interesting for instance, production, transport, imports and exports, retail, textiles, and so on.

Therefore, before you can appreciate what it takes to make money, you need to understand the definition of being rich. Once you have grasped this, you are on your way to making money. Be creative.

Entrepreneurial skills come through Ambition and hard work.

The late Aristotle Onassis, the most famous shipping magnate of the 20th century and the founder of Olympic Airways (today Olympic Airlines), is a good example of a self-made millionaire (when he died he was a billionaire).

Even Aristotle Onassis formulated money-spinning strategies as a child. On one occasion, it is said, the school stationery shop burnt down. Onassis bought the damaged pencils from the school at a discounted price and paid for two new sharpeners. With the help of a school friend, they sharpened the damaged pencils. Then they sold them to their school friends for very low prices, making a profit.

Born in Smyrna, the son of a wealthy Greek trader and a Turkish citizen in what was then the Ottoman Empire (now Izmir, Turkey), he and his family fled to Greece as refugees in1922. A year later, at the age of 17, Onassis set off for South America, where he allegedly worked as a dishwasher.

However, he had a burning desire to make money. Within three years, he had turned his own fortunes around. Various forms of tobacco paved the way to this fast start in the millionaire stakes. By 1932, Onassis had become an excellent businessman, owning commercial ships, tankers, and whalers right around the world. His estimated wealth in 1956 was $300 million. By the time he died in 1975, it was impossible to calculate exactly how much he was worth. His inestimable fortune passed to his only surviving child, Christina.

Neither inherited wealth nor the best academic degree guarantees or affords you the greatest wealth. Even though some families earn at the higher end of the income spectrum, still they are not rich - why? Because they have no appreciative financial assets to their name.

They may have no investments and very few savings. They may own a few expensive cars but cars, like many other items, are perishable and waste away over time unless they are classic models. In other words their value depreciates. Real millionaires are self-reliant. They normally have the ability to continue living their current lifestyles for many years. They do not rely on other people for their wages, and have strong entrepreneurial skills.

High consumption families spend money on material goods. Change your and your family's lifestyles.

TOP TIP

The vast majority of millionaires also pay for the best financial advice. They employ accountants and advisors from the top end of their professions. They look for quality in services. There's no point thinking about becoming rich if you have no concept of what this entails. Once you understand and appreciate this, you are on your way to making money work for you.

That's a lot better than being stuck on a grindstone, working just to make ends meet. You can start up a business in the hope of making money, and see it become relatively successful in the short term, with good profit margins. However, this is not enough to ensure that you reap wealth consistently in the long term.

Many people make the mistake of separating their work from their personal spending habits. Why is this so important? Simple. You can earn or accumulate large profit margins from your business but, if your lifestyle choice is to spend and live lavishly, you will never save any substantial wealth. Your leisure pursuits may swallow up the profits from your business. So be careful. Also if you do start up a business make sure you get in the right staff, especially the right managers.

The Burger story

I know one friend Mr. Henderson. He is a nice chap and started off in a burger shop making burgers. Mr Henderson made many burgers and his productivity was high. He had been making burgers on the shop floor for a long time. He loved burgers so he took great care and pride in making them. He also liked to be on the shop floor and enjoyed the sound of the till when customers came in. He was however, always stressed and sent out negative vibes to other co-workers. But he was good at making burgers.

Then one day the senior manager decided that it was time that Mr Henderson should be promoted because he had been making burgers for years. Mr Henderson did not have any training to be a manager. He was offered a managerial position and was very happy. So he became a manager. The senior manager left Mr Henderson to manage his business and went off. But Mr Henderson could not think off anything except making burgers. So instead of considering the strategic direction of his bosses' company and the operational, staff, advertising and marketing decisions, instead he decided to jump into the shop floor everyday and help out to make the burgers. The shop floor was his comfort-zone.

When new staff joined the burger shop Mr Henderson refused to teach them how to make good burgers. If staff

Self-employed people have a better a chance statistically of becoming millionaires.

TOP TIP

made good burgers Mr. Henderson would always complain that he in fact made the best burgers. When the senior manager occasionally asked for feedback about staff, Mr. Henderson would tell the senior manager that by far he was the best person to make burgers. This frustrated everyone and staff began to lose respect for Mr. Henderson and many started to look for opportunities outside the burger shop. After a few months Mr. Henderson was still making burgers.

The senior boss handled the financial and some strategic operations relating to his business with very little help from Mr. Henderson. The business remained afloat.

Unfortunately Mr. Henderson never understood the wider implications of his behaviour and possibly the senior manager didn't either because he was too busy.

If Mr. Henderson had been business-minded he would have realised that a lot of people who want to make burgers do that as a sideline. They know how to make burgers and those staff who have experience working in other burger shops can actually bring a refreshingly new way of looking and thinking and working to make burgers. What he should have done, is delegate effectively so that the junior staff could take on their own responsibilities, while

Mr. Henderson could have concentrated on expansion and new ideas.

Mr. Henderson could have set up another business within the burger sector to stave off competitors. He could have concentrated on introducing a whole new range of foods in line with current market conditions. Mr. Henderson could have offered new packages to customers. He could have looked at the costs elements of burgers. Indeed Mr. Henderson could have concentrated on taking the business a step further and generating more money. Unfortunately he didn't do that and who suffered at the end? Well no one really. Not even the senior manager because he was used to the status quo and didn't realise all the missed opportunities.

In the interim other competitors came on the scene and the business hadn't accounted for this rise in burger shops just a few doors away from them. Other competitors began stealing the shops customers and staff began to leave. But Mr. Henderson continued to make burgers. One acquaintance I saw recently told me that Mr. Henderson is still making burgers and the senior manager decided to put Mr. Henderson back onto the shop floor where he worked the best and where he enjoyed making burgers and surprisingly now also likes the customers that come into the shop.

Moral: get the right staff.

Chapter 7

Choosing The Right Business

MANY SUCCESSFUL MILLIONAIRES are educated to degree level and higher. But there are also a sizeable number of millionaires who made their money without obtaining any academic degree.

Keep in mind, the longer you stay on the education ladder, the more time you waste off the money ladder. Many millionaires get onto this ladder earlier than their counterpart college/university peers do.

Many millionaires will tell you it wasn't easy making that first million. Perhaps it was a hard road to travel, and they may have been knocked down along the way, but it was their own inner drive that kept them going. Keep yourself motivated. If you get criticized for following your dreams and ambitions don't be disheartened.

Successful people have common traits, for instance drive, ambition, an innate ability to move on and overcome defeatism and look forward to the future and a real genuine belief that they will be successful. Most successful millionaires are passionate about their work. They believe in their dream.

Many millionaires, despite having millions in their bank account, continue to invest the same hours in their work not because they need to, but because they enjoy what they are doing. Find something you are good at, interested in or passionate about. Millionaires get wholeheartedly behind the product or service they are offering, and this motivates them to make more money.

Find out what you are good at. Then ask yourself if you can make money from this skill. Maybe you like cooking. Consider a restaurant, or a food franchise. Perhaps you like working with interior design. Could you make money from that? When you already have a hobby or pastime that you are passionate about it can act as the first stepping-stone towards a business venture.

Money can be made from specialising in business, looking out for niche-market opportunities. Can you forecast trends? Do some research. Where do you think the economy will be heading in five years' time? What kinds of products will people require? As the European Union opens up, more and more people are settling in the UK. They will need legal advice, which means lawyers will be in a position to offer a lucrative service.

You can only make money if others make for you.

TOP TIP

What other consequences will flow from this? The housing market may benefit. People from abroad may be attracted to major cities such as London, Birmingham, and Manchester. These could be good places to invest in real estate. Because of booming house prices, Britain now has a large percentage of millionaires, especially in the London region.

The opening of the EU works two ways. Look around carefully. You might find a niche in tourism, education, or fast food in Eastern Europe, Italy or Austria. Maybe there's a new market for sports gear, clubbing, or ski poles made in a new kind of material.

Don't be lazy. Honestly ask yourself, have you ever been called this? If so then ask how often? If the answer covers more than the fingers of one hand, there maybe a grain of truth in this remark. When you've finally managed to get yourself into the frame of mind for getting rich, you have to persist in that goal.

You need to formulate a plan. Instead of wasting time lounging around in front of the TV, or down at the local pub, spend your time more profitably on constructive planning and steps that could activate a new kind of lifestyle.

Be disciplined and avoid bad habits. Idleness doesn't get you anywhere except probably to your bed and your sofa. Life is for the living. When you die, you will sleep forever.

There is No Golden Goose

Flamboyant entrepreneur, Richard Branson is one of the richest people in the UK. His business mind went into gear at the age of 16, when he published a student magazine. He didn't go on to graduate school. Instead, he worked as a bus driver at weekends until he had enough money to rent a bookshop in Camden, London.

This was the cornerstone of his immense wealth. Branson's first publishing project was Paul Hamlyn Associates. It specialized in cheap, popular works, especially art, travel, and cooking. He sold his interest to IPC in 1964. In 1970, the now famous Virgin brand began as a mail order venture selling discount records that he and his friend, Nik Powell worked on. Soon after opening a record store on Oxford Street, London, Branson began a recording label in 1972, Virgin Records. This was to be the first major success for the British entrepreneur as he started the label with a hit record.

Calculate in advance what you expect to spend each month. Budget wisely.

TOP TIP

The instrumental artist Mike Oldfield's "Tubular Bells" released in 1973 was a cash cow for Branson's Virgin Records. Branson went on to set up Octopus Publishing Group, and in 1987 he sold this business for £535 million. The Virgin Records Group was sold in 1992 to Thorn EMI for $1 billion USD.

Whole stacks of businesses throughout the world now wear the Virgin name, and there will probably be more to come. Branson is always looking for an interesting business to start up.

Richard Branson didn't have a golden goose. Even though he seems to have a lot of fun, he got where he is with planning and budgeting. When you get the planning right, then you can have some fun! So let's get down to the basics of it. You need to plan and budget to become rich. This means planning on a weekly, monthly, or even a yearly basis.

You need to calculate, in advance, where you expect your money to go for instance on a mortgage, food, clothes, etc. Allocate a ceiling figure, which you can aim to stick to. For instance when you plan to spend £300 for food per month, budget down to £250 and then stick to it.

Think of ways to help you stick to your targets. Save money by buying food in 'bulk' it's cheaper and more cost effective.

Be less busy. Being busy could potentially cost you MORE money! When you live a fast paced lifestyle, it is surprising how much inconvenience this causes, not to mention the spiraling amount of money that you spend to actually save time. For instance, when you work a few extra hours in evenings as overtime, do you spend half of that on takeaway food? It doesn't make sense.

When you want to make money, the rule is to also investigate your lifestyle and find out where you can make cutbacks to help you 'save'. Successful, wealthy individuals budget wisely. They know where they spend their money.

Some people are compulsive shoppers. That is, they are addicted to spending money on what they think are 'bargains'. They spend hours and hours shopping for items that they do not actually need, often for them to lurk at the back of their cupboards unused. Likewise, they often purchase on credit to fund their extravagant lifestyles, imagining that people will believe their wealth from the status of their designer label. Recognise if you are one of these people and act upon it. The curse of contemporary times is the saying 'I shop. Therefore I am'.

Poor management will cripple any business you set up and/or prevent it from achieving success.

TOP TIP

Wealthy individuals have accountants to keep track of where their money is spent. If you can't afford an accountant, learn some basic accounting. This will be a useful tool if you want to become and remain wealthy. As boring as it may seem, accounting, or at least some level of financial competency, is a 'must-have' skill.

A lack of financial planning eats up your ability to accumulate wealth. Make a habit of keeping accurate records of your expenses. Even when you don't have time to do this every day, keep all your receipts in a box, and make time every week to calculate how much you have spent. When you purchase goods, foodstuffs or receive a service from someone, always ask for a receipt. To change habits is difficult. Yet when you make that break, you are well on your way to becoming rich.

People who spend heavily on material objects fall into a trap. They have no real money left to invest. Even when they hold down prosperous jobs, there is a possibility that the market might change and therefore their means of making a living. If you lost your job, could you still afford to live the same lifestyle?

Have a careful look at your daily expenses, and see where you can save money. Ask yourself whether you spend on impulse? Do you really need that new sofa or cooker now? Can you wait to buy it during the sales? Scrimp and save, save, save. You know the saying, "save your pennies for a rainy day".

Learn to bargain, barter, haggle, and negotiate prices. Look around the market. If you want to buy a cooker or any other item - would you normally go to a high street shop you are familiar with because of their advertising? Or would you contact a few shops to look at their offers? Do you know what type of model you are looking for?

Always get at least three to four quotations before you buy, and wait until you can get the best price. Consider how much time and money you waste trying to find bargains - do you really have that much spare time? Look hard at the item you are thinking about buying. Is it a financial asset, or will it depreciate? Take time to find the best deal. It may be worthwhile, but if you want a top of the range stereo (a depreciating asset), it may not be worth the time spent hunting down the best priced product.

Some households have more than one car. Ask yourself how many cars do you really need. Cut back so that you can save money on road taxes and insurance. A very high consumption household may affect children negatively. Consider the example you are setting. They learn about thrift or excessive spending from their parents. Unless they are taught self-discipline, they will not learn to appreciate wealth, as they will be used to careless spending.

If you work in a high paced job and work long hours, you may feel that you have no time to plan financially. Well, someone needs to. If your partner was not working, would he or she be able to take on the responsibility of keeping a check on expenses and outgoings?

If not, then you will have to make time to analyze your expenditure. When you keep a record, you can see at a glance where your money is going. People who are serious about making money tend to plan, and will make time for this activity. If you want to get rich quickly, get yourself into this mind-set.

You don't need to spend hundreds of hours a month doing accounts. Even a few hours a month can make a real difference. For instance instead of watching TV one week why not devote that time to planning and investing? You won't become rich overnight, but you will definitely be on your way to making money. Also, if you decide to make cutbacks, you need to continue this steadily over a number of months and years. You have to be gutsy and stick to your aim of making money.

Avoid the temptations along the way and stick to your saving plan. Your friends may be wearing the latest fashion accessories, shoes or handbags, but persevere and try and save your money rather than rushing out to copy them. Also, avoid compulsive discount shopping. Remember once you are rich you can comfortably buy whatever you want in moderation of course.

Millionaires tend to hire the best staff. They look for people with the best qualifications because they can then use their skills to benefit their organization. When you are thinking of investing or hiring an accountant or going to meet with a bank advisor or an investment broker for advice on how best to save, interview them as if you are hiring a member of staff. Check their credentials, check their record of 'success' - don't be shy of asking questions. Ultimately, the final investment decision rests with you.

Do you believe in fairytales?

Lucky Aladdin who had a genie who granted him wishes. And what about little Cinders who kept cleaning away until she was rescued by her prince and lived happily ever

Be prepared to sacrifice your leisure time.

TOP TIP

after in a fairytale castle. These rags to riches stories teach us some good lessons. Persistence and faith will help you get rich. Don't give up. Believe in yourself and you will become rich.

If you have read any fairytales, you have probably noticed most of them have happy endings. If you haven't read any read some, so that you understand what they are saying. Whether it is Aladdin or Cinderella, we love these characters because they are a reflection of us. Deep down we all want security for ourselves and our family.

Get a Life

Learn to create MORE time. You don't have enough time to make extra money? Ask a millionaire or someone aspiring successfully to that goal and they will probably give you a simple answer 'Make Time'.

You don't have to be a great mathematician to work out how many months there are in a year: 12. That's a long time. Let's break down that figure further so you can appreciate just how much time you have. 12 months a year is 52 weeks. That's 365 days. On average, people in the UK work 40 hours per week. That's an average eight hours a day, with weekends free. The rich work double that amount of time. The average millionaire works 80 hours or more per week, and that's every week.

It does not require a magical formula to work out that the millionaire has turned his 12 months into 24 months. That time is spent making money and even having time for leisure pursuits. The culture of working long hours is embedded into the culture of the Asian sub-continent.

You can use the millionaire checklist below to help you manage your time. Even if you are not ready yet to start up your own business, you can still make time to start planning your second income.

Keep a record calculating the hours spent on common tasks. This will help you see at a glance roughly on average how many hours are spent on household chores, socializing, working, TV etc.

Remember it may be difficult in the beginning to keep a record, but you have to do it. Otherwise, you will not know where your time is going. You can 'make time' by cutting down on unnecessary activities. You don't have to cut non-essentials completely out of your life. After all, it's good to watch TV now and again to stimulate the mind. Nor is it

Don't be afraid to take calculated risks.

TOP TIP

healthy to cut yourself off from the world and your friends, but do ask yourself do you really need to 'go-out' every weekend. And it's not necessary to answer every single call and unsolicited mail! You could invest that time in making money instead.

When you decide you actually do have a millionaire mind-set (and a strongly disciplined work-ethic), you can get started.

Don't be embarrassed about putting in extra hours to better your future or that of your family. You will feel much better in later years when you invest the time now. Also remember that you can become a millionaire at any age. Just by working 2 extra hours a day (1 hour in the morning and 1 hour in the evening) you can notch up 10 hours a week that's an amazing 40 hours a month. This calculates to an extra 3 months in the year. So instead of your years being 12 months, it actually becomes 15 months. Those hours can be spent on your money-making ideas and projects even if you are employed.

Many millionaires don't just work an extra 2 hours a day they also work on weekends on average of 16 hours - now you do the maths!

Chapter 8

Know Where You Are Going

People who are serious about making money and succeeding in life have plans, whether they are on paper or in their minds. They have a 'road map' for the future. Too often people give up at the first sign of trouble or set back. Be prepared to sacrifice leisure time if you want to make that first million. Sleep but don't overdo it unless you absolutely need to. Life is for living, not sleeping.

They also have aims and objectives and are not afraid of taking risks along the way. They devise and use tools to help them on their journey to success. Get into the habit of making a plan and you will become successful in many areas of your life.

Most people don't really know what they want. It's plain good sense to have some aims. Isn't it about time you took out a few minutes a day for planning? Call it 'me time' and think about where you hope or expect to be, in say a year's time. Your idea of wealth will also influence whether or not you will become a millionaire. Whether wealth brings you happiness or unhappiness depends on your view of the world. If you think money is 'evil' then you might as well stop your project of making a million.

Think about how much money you want in 12 months' time. Write down the figure on a piece of paper and put it somewhere you can access it easily every week. When you are earning £12,000 a year then in 12 months' time you should aim for at least £24,000.

The third step in becoming wealthy is to learn how you want to achieve that goal. Will you be taking on a second job because you are not yet ready to start up your own business? Perhaps you have a partner who also earns the same amount as you. When you combine your wages, you can both aim to double that amount next year. In two years, how much money do you expect to have made? Write down the amount. Remember, as your '0' digits grow you will know that you are making money and on the road to success.

However, if you really want to kick-start yourself into making money for yourself, set up your own business. Of course, you need to have an idea for a product, or provide a service that will be lucrative and in tune with the market conditions. To make a million you need vision. Inspiration and passion are key ingredients to success. Ask yourself questions, including: Is there a gap in the market?

Poor quality staff cost you more money in the long run. Poor results will follow, in time.

TOP TIP

Visualise how your new business will look and the money coming in then get started to make the dream come alive. That's what millionaires do.

You may already have savings that you can use to start up your businesses. If not, you need to start saving. Learn the tips in this book to make money work for you. Have a business plan. There's no point wasting months or even years designing this plan. Set yourself a deadline. You may need to borrow some money to help get you started. If the bank (the traditional money lending institution) does not believe your money-making idea and turns you down for a loan, don't let that stop you from looking to other places to raise money, for instance your friends and family could be your next port of call.

Getting a franchise is one way to go. According to Entrepreneur magazine, the hottest franchise trends for 2004 were in the following areas:

New Opportunities:

- Specialty ice cream. Sugar remains a strong seller, especially in ice cream. The wider range of products available fuels the growth here, including organic, and the advent of personalised sprinkles, sweets and other such items.

- Coffee. It started way back in the 1900s and is steaming ahead after a lull in the 70s and 80s. Coffee is a strong franchise category, especially when the coffee house can offer something unique, such as jazz or soup.

- Health and fitness. Franchises for these have been around for a long time. However, the fitness club has become the new leisure space. There are also big openings for women-only centres, especially when crèche facilities are offered.

- Children's products and services. Parents, especially when they both have careers, need extra education for their children. They also need fitness programmes, creative outlets such as dance or music, self-development and entertainment.

- Technology. Technological services, especially computer training and consulting, have moved into a new stage of development after a quiet period. People and businesses need advice on how to work their equipment and what to buy or upgrade to, including ISP and broadband services.

You can generate wealth from projects you actually 'enjoy' doing.

TOP TIP

- Home improvement. People keep spending on their homes. The home improvement area recorded almost 15% growth in 2003, and looks like coming in with even stronger growth in the latest figures. Remodelling, windows and double-glazing, conservatories, painting and lighting are high on the list. This means that professional electricians, builders, handymen and lighting specialists have a high market value.
- Income Tax. This is an ever-growing area and it's not likely to fade away in a hurry. Franchises for preparing tax returns have been around for years. However, the increasing complexities of tax laws have bewildered the average taxpayer. That factor, coupled with advances in IT software, mean that tax services can be provided more easily and efficiently than ever before so long as the tax consultant knows his or her way round the appropriate tax software.
- Business consulting and mentoring. The growth in all kinds of consulting, counselling, and mentoring services is driven by small businesses that need answers but don't have anywhere.

If you want to check out an up-to-date 2007 list of hundreds of franchise possibilities visit

www.franchiseopportunities.com/

Many of the areas specified above have flourished over the years. To start anything off requires capital. Be creative and look for alternative ways to raise money. Can you raise money from your bank? Is there a venture capitalist that believes in your idea and is willing to back you in return for a cut in the profits?

Whatever you do, don't get yourself into huge debt before you've taken the first leap into the 'making money route'. Get as much advice as you possibly can. And only borrow the money if you really need to.

Learn from what they have to say but don't let constructive criticism become confused with personal attacks. Certainly, you will come across personal attacks throughout your life, but rise above them. Millionaires made their money through hard work and patience. They overcame obstacles and continued in their belief and ambition of becoming rich. Don't expect an easy ride unless you are very lucky.

When you have a passion and you believe you can succeed, you will do so. Keep the dream alive and believe in yourself. With that picture in mind, do your research thoroughly.

This is no time to be resting. When you die, you will sleep forever.

TOP TIP

There's no point offering a product and service without a target clientele or consumer base for it. On the other hand, don't be put off any idea until you are sure there is no end user for it.

Sometimes millionaires have made their money from highly unusual, not so orthodox ventures that others said had no potential. If you're passionate about a hobby, turn it into a money-spinner. People have made millions from breeding worms and selling dirt, virtual boyfriends and cuddling strangers (legitimately), pooper-scoopers and Halloween doggie costumes.

Methods that are more orthodox have made billionaires of millionaires. For instance look at the example of Lakshmi Mittal. Although not a self-made millionaire, his father actually was already in the steel business, his story is a good example of how wealth can be quadrupled if you have the right business acumen.

Mittal loved steel, he simply couldn't get enough of it. Whilst his father was driving the business forward he studied accountancy before taking over the reigns himself.

He then went on to build an empire of steel by recognizing the economic prosperity and demand for steel from India and China.

Other billionaire charmers include the Hinduja brothers. The name Hinduja has become a global household name. The four brothers, Srichand, Gopichand, Prakash and Ashok, inherited their commercial kingdom but did not squander its fortunes, as so happens. Instead using their wit and business acumen they turned this kingdom into a mega-empire.

At the heart of Hinduja-land is commerce: trading and banking. The group has also expanded into diverse and related areas including media and communications and holds stakes in many other business ventures. If you think Disneyland, think Hinduja-land.

Key areas, where millionaires (predominately from the Asian community) have made their money include pharmaceuticals, food, industry, computers, telecoms, hotels, and cash and carry,import and export. Just pay a visit to some of the textile towns in the UK or London's East End and you will see that the Asian communities have been at the forefront of this business.

Chapter 9

A Definite Plan Of Action

THOSE PEOPLE who society views as wealthy tend to be celebrities. Their images stick in our mind and distort our perceptions of who and what wealth really defines. In reality, often these figures lead high-consumption lifestyles that are fed by increasingly alarming debts. The frequency with which entertainers and athletes file for bankruptcy is one indication of the difference between those whom we perceive to be wealthy and those who actually are wealthy.

The story is not all gloom and doom however. Some clever celebrities have managed to become multi-millionaires through hard work. And the secret to their success? They have learnt how to handle and invest their money wisely. Most millionaires have mastered the art of spending well below, and certainly not in excess of what they earn. They are less likely to squander funds on depreciable assets and frequently live modestly, even though their net worth may be quite high. Having respect for money is essential. If you can't respect it - it won't respect you.

Their stories reflect everything we have learnt up to this point. Careful management of their funds, investing their time and wealth wisely, and the golden rule; having self-confidence and belief in the ability to succeed. The mind is a powerful tool that will help or hinder you along the path to making your dreams come true.

Now get a note pad and felt tip pen. You need to develop and formulate a plan of action. If you don't have this, you will waste precious time. A plan is the evidence and reflection of your goals and aspirations. Regard it as a map to help you on your journey.

Recall how we talked about envisioning where you wish to be in, say, 3 years' time, 6 years, and 9 years. Approach this with a definite belief that you can achieve your dreams; otherwise you can forget about making money. Also the more money you accumulate the more you will attract. As you save and watch your wealth grow your confidence and outlook on life will change. You will attract more wealth and more opportunities will open to you. This is a fact of life. That's why children of rich parents tend to start on a good standing in life - they have the opportunities mapped out for them. What may worry the mind of someone from a non-wealthy family may occupy the mind of someone from a wealthy family but the differences in how they deal with it depends on what opportunities they have open to them.

Learn basic accounting skills.

TOP TIP

You may be surprised at the amount of money you can actually save through relatively minor changes to your lifestyle. Stop buying on credit. There may be times when you may need to, but really try and think two, three, four times before you consider using credit. It's a guaranteed way to lose money. Think of the huge interest that you will also have to pay on top of the principal loan.

Myths about becoming a millionaire

You don't need thousands and thousands of pounds to get started on the way to becoming a millionaire. If you are already in a job, you are lucky because you can start the process of making yourself rich from here.

Even when you have a full time day job, you may decide to take up an evening job to save that initial pool of seed money to invest in appreciating assets. The money will grow as your investment (when market conditions are right) gathers profits. Also if you have a partner, combine your income with theirs, you then have an even better chance of quickly amassing more money.

Remember the key is balance: work hard, play hard.

Keep some semblance of normality. Some people have boring and unfulfilling jobs so they spend an equal amount of time trying to drown that dissatisfaction. But millionaires and those who are passionate about their work will spend their free time working on projects that they are passionate about. So work and play can become one. It is wonderful if your passion is also bringing you money.

You can't make millions when you don't have an idea. So get your thinking cap on and think of a unique service or product you can provide.

Once you have made your seed money, you can comfortably place it in the hands of an FDIC insured bank, a mutual fund company, or a reputable individual such as a licensed stockbroker. Use other talented people to make money on your behalf. But be careful to do the research properly before handing your money to someone else.

One area you may not have considered is litigation. It could actually cost you a lot of money and eat into your wealth. In today's society the rate of litigation is phenomenally increasing. The USA bug to sue and be sued is now also making its mark in the UK. Every year, countless individuals go through the motions of divorce, partnership break-ups and resolving such disputes means they often end up in court.

Keep your eyes open for bargains and learn to barter and haggle.

TOP TIP

Partnerships go wrong. Businesses start up and then one partner may decide he or she wants out. Someone may come into your shop and slip. They injure themselves. Before you know it you could be facing a personal injury claim.

Litigation can arise from many different and unexpected areas of business. If you are not careful you could find yourself paying out thousands of pounds in damages. So if you do come across a potential problem ensure you get good legal advice.

Tricks of the Trade

You don't need a magician to make your dreams come true Thinking about making money is one thing. Actually making it is something else. Don't be shy. Unless you win the lottery or inherit money, you won't become a millionaire overnight.

Do write down your ideal target, a target that is more than a million. Then ask yourself how you are going to achieve it. Write your thoughts down. Break this analysis down into practical steps, and resolve to follow them one by one.

When you want to make money quickly, you also need to invest in your health. You can't make money when you are ill. So eat things that will give you sustenance, such as coriander, which has highly therapeutic properties.

Avoid heavy meals. Eat bite-size snacks. Eat at least one good meal at lunchtime or in the evening, but not too late at night. Otherwise you will find it difficult to sleep. Get proper nourishment. That means lots of fruit, vegetables, and a variety of nutritional foods. Detox frequently. Drink the purest water you can afford lots of it every day.

Eating and drinking healthily will keep your body in optimum condition. You will need a healthy attitude psychologically, but also physical strength if you want to become wealthy.

What's the point of working hard to make a good future for yourself if you eat unhealthily and are killing yourself by drinking alcohol and/or smoking cigarettes? The choice is up to you. Health is wealth. Wealth is health. The two are like lovers. When you have wealth you are in a powerful position you have much more control of your life and your destinies. The more money you accumulate, the more opportunity you have to better your lifestyle and that of your dependants. Poverty can make people extremely depressed and stressed not because they are inherently like that but because they can't afford to do the things money can buy.

> The secret of wealth actually lies within you. All you have to do is tap into that inner power.
>
> **TOP TIP**

As long as you're not afraid of hard work, it's not difficult to make a million. Hundreds of millionaires never inherited a penny. However, some of them did learn a strong work discipline from their parents, while others learned to be frugal from them.

These ingredients discipline and thrift are the basis of success. They will help you on the road to becoming not just a millionaire but also a multimillionaire. It's always difficult to make that first million, as many of the millionaires told me. But once you've made that first million, it's easy to make more. Also learn to tap into the power of your mind and you will start to achieve your goals.

The secret of wealth actually lies within you. All you have to do is tap into that inner power. Then you can unleash it and make it work for you. First, though, you need to be committed, and then you have to get started. Make time to think about how you are going to achieve your goal of making a million pounds. Learn to set aside at least 15 minutes a day and concentrate on your money making ideas. You will be surprised at what you can achieve over the space of just one month. progress

Even when you're in a poverty rut or feel that you could be much better off, don't waste time blaming your circumstances, environment, or parents. You can divert that precious time and energy into a resource right away by helping yourself to get on that path of making money.

It won't always be an easy ride. At the same time, you need to stay positive. Keep your hope and passion alive, whatever anyone else says. Your dreams are attainable when you learn a few simple techniques.

Follow the rules in this book and you will be well on your way to understanding the 'tricks of the trade'. You might even kick yourself for not learning these tricks earlier. These are good tricks! And everything advised in this book is ethical.

Once you master the technique of making money and then watching it grow, you might feel let down or angry because you have wasted so much time getting onto the money making ladder. Once again, don't fret. Don't blame yourself, parents or circumstances for being poor. Just grasp the bull by the horns and get going. Time is precious. Time wasted is no good to you.

> Poor management will cripple any business you set up and/or prevent it from achieving success.
>
> **TOP TIP**

Skills that help you make money can also be applied to other areas of your life including health and personal relationships. By just using the key tips in this book, you can succeed in whatever you choose to do. Better still, you can apply them to other areas of your life. For instance, you can become a better lover or a better student.

The first step to making money is to brave it and set up your own business - become self-employed. Even if you are petrified of going it alone, think again. Unless you have the guts to go out there and set up on your own, you are unlikely to become a millionaire.

The millionaires covered in this book are entrepreneurs. Each of them has made a point of running their 'own show'. Look at Stelios Haji-Ioannou, who saw a gap in the market in 1995 and set up the airline EasyJet. He amassed an estimated $1.4 billion from this venture.

Millionaires pull the strings. They employ other people to work for them. They invest money in assets that appreciate over time, and which in turn make more money for them. As explained earlier, you don't even need an advanced education to make money but if you do, then you can use it to your own advantage.

If you have some formal education that is brilliant, but only if you can use it to your advantage - to make money. Any education is better than no education. You have an added edge over your contemporaries when you have the know-how. However, education is not an essential tool for making money. Indeed there are many millionaires who never graduated academically and still made millions. If you are studying and educating yourself then at least select courses that are relevant to help you making money, opt for subjects such as Accounting, Maths and English. Remember though, education is useless when you don't know how to apply the principles you have learned.

Also the more time you spend 'in-education' the less time you have to make money. This shouldn't put you off studying because graduates notch the top jobs in many companies because they have the training and skills to meet the demands of the market-forces, but suffice to note that staying in education means you will not be making money unless you have a money-making project as a side-line. Many non-graduates are indeed privileged in one way because they have more time to divert their attention to money-making ideas and accumulating wealth.

The key to lifelong success is continuing self-improvement. Learn from books, CDs, newspapers. Attend lectures and seminars. Keep abreast of current affairs. You don't have to sit exams, but keep learning new

Have a plan it will save you time and money.

TOP TIP

things, especially about the business and marketplace you are working in. The more you learn the more knowledge you have to expand and improve your business. You can hopefully one day multiply your wealth from a million to millions.

Once you are rich you then have the luxury of employing the best brains in the business. Successful and wealthy people tend to hire the best brains, because they know how these educated class of people can make money for them. A millionaire must have the ability to look after his affairs, understand his wealth and employ those who share his drive.

Millionaires are becoming younger and there are more of them now than there were only a few years ago. With the recent phenomenal rise in the property market in particular, it opened up an avenue for making money that is accessible to all, regardless of age and prior experience. Some of these property millionaires may have inherited the wealth; others inadvertently became millionaires because of the property boom.

New avenues are opening up all the time and millionaires are making their money in all sorts of diverse markets. Information technology and mass communication systems have opened the door for everyone to get out there and make money. The worldwide web has also really opened up the market to offer a product to a global audience.

Aside from the technical revolution of the Internet, it has opened up an ocean of wealth for retailers. The Internet's knock-on effects have created a whole host of millionaires who provide e-solutions and other services. The global economy is moving faster than ever, bringing many more markets to explore. With the rising economies of India, China and Africa, the world is about to open up even more possibilities for making wealth.

Even if you don't have the guts to get out there and start up on your own business, you can still find valuable tips in this book. They will help you to change your perspective on how you approach money, both now and in the long term.

It may help you to decide what your long-term priorities are to live in luxury now, or save for the future? There may never be a good time to start to make money. You might be tempted to keep putting off your money making projects because you are too busy.

Establish whether there is a client base for your target audience.

TOP TIP

We hear it all the time: 'I have got a house full of kids to look after', 'I have a day job and am absolutely exhausted after that', 'Maybe when I am on vacation I will start on the projects'. But days turn into weeks, and weeks into months. You don't need to be a doctor of medicine or an accountant to earn money.

People have made their money from spotting gaps in the market and providing services and goods from which they have then reaped the benefits. They can then afford to sit back (even though they don't) and watch their empires generate money for the future.

When you clean and de-clutter your mind and environment, you help release energy so that it can flow freely. You can tap into this energy subconsciously. It will help you think creatively and free your mind up, allowing you to think more clearly and keep you focused.

You will also need to stay organised. A disorganized approach to your project will cause problems. Keep a file or two to tidy away any paperwork at the end of the day.

Get into a routine to keep documents in an orderly fashion. Whether you tidy up fortnightly, monthly, or even daily, make this a good habit. That's another step in becoming a millionaire.

Chapter 10

Cut Back Your Expenses

IT'S OK TO MAKE substantial cutbacks and downsize your existing consumption habits to save money. Start soon, so that you can start adding to the pool of money, which you can then use to invest into new businesses. Learn the meaning of the following words and learn how to apply them: ASSET, EXPENSE, LIABILITY, EQUITY, SAVING. This book will teach you to understand what these terms mean.

If you went to a bank and they turned you down for - loan to start up your new business, don't be upset and angry, and don't give up. Being rejected can teach you a few useful lessons. It may even motivate you to work harder.

Remember, expenses can kill a business so when you start out keep a constant eye on expenditure with a view to keeping all costs down. For instance, instead of employing 3-4 members of staff with poor productivity or limited qualifications, invest in 1-2 good high-quality ones whose productivity is high. You might not need top education, but ensure your staff receive the best training. This will not only save you money but will help your business get on the right track.

Ask yourself questions like whether you want to offer credit? How likely is it that people will pay on time? There is a very real danger to small businesses of payments never being recovered. Cover yourself by asking for payments up-front. That way, you know exactly where you stand. It means you have control and peace of mind because you don't have to waste time, effort and money chasing payments.

There is no guarantee that you will see profits straight away. In fact, you could wait for several months before you see any money. Too often people give up at the first sign of trouble. You have to persevere.

On the way to getting rich, you will definitely sacrifice your leisure hours, unless you are very, very lucky. Indeed, you may lose a lot of quality time with your family and friends. Can you stand being accused of selfishness and greed? It gets worse. You may be accused of being self-centred and only interested in material possessions. But persevere. The fact you have children, family or additional responsibilities may actually motivate you to work harder and earn more.

Brush up your creative skills you will need plenty of them to make money.

TOP TIP

Perhaps you already hold these values while you work for someone else. Good. That means when you decide to move on to setting up on your own, it will not be difficult to transfer these skills and your motivation into your own business.

In this book my attention is on self-made millionaires. Whatever the medium through which they made their money, be it in textiles, food, shipping or other services and products, certain personality traits win through.

These characteristics are explored further throughout this book. You already know that they are careful with their resources, thrifty, good at saving, and make a practice of living below their means. They also believe in their dream, confront obstacles head-on, and use initiative and persistence in continuing on to their ultimate aim. If you are aspiring to become a millionaire don't become 'stingy Scrooge'. No one likes an overly miserly person. Instead learn to save and use your money wisely and responsibly.

What are the negatives you might meet on your journey to make a million pounds? On the road, you might hear people saying, 'What you are doing is pointless and useless', 'Look at us, we make money every day'. Are you convinced?

You can tell yourself (or ask them), 'OK, so you're making money today, and probably even tomorrow and the day after that, but how long can you continue? Just who are you making money for? Is it for yourself good! Or is it for someone else?!' Self employed people are statistically more likely to become millionaires than those who merely work for someone else.

Now, what does being wealthy mean for you? How would you interpret the word, wealth? One man thinks that being rich means having enough money to party every night in luxury, while another thinks that being rich means he can support and look after his loved ones in comfort, without having to worry about paying a mortgage.

Wealth is intrinsically linked to being happy. When someone thinks of becoming a millionaire, they often have a picture in their head of happiness. They may believe that money equates to sheer happiness, and to the ending of all troubles. This is true. Well, it can be. Some people think that spiritual wealth is more valuable than material gains. But there is no denying that wealth can bring happiness whether it is spiritual or material.

However, when you have high spiritual ideals, you may want enough money to set up an orphanage, a monastery

Engender a positive attitude to life.

TOP TIP

for prayer, or a shelter for the homeless. Many entrepreneurs donate money to charity. They gain enormous satisfaction from knowing that their money is being used to help the poor and needy at home, or in the developing world. One multi-millionaire who is well known for his generosity is Sir Gulam Noon. He was knighted during the Queen's birthday honours in 2002 for 'services to industry'.

Sir Ghulam, whose Indian "ready meals" empire is worth an estimated £100 million, began his career in Mumbai at the age of 17 and later moved to the UK where his businesses have grown into some of the most successful companies in the sector.

Noon set up his sweet company in 1973. By 1989, he had moved his interests into curry production. The company now supplies major restaurant and other outlets.

Noon is on the board of Cancer Research UK, the British Food Trust, Maimonides Foundation, the Memorial Gates Trust and Arpana Charitable Trust. Noon founded the Noon Foundation, with a major donation of £4 million from his personal assets in 1955.

The Foundation has given grants to a range of multi-faith and multi-cultural projects in the UK and India.

Money is a form of energy. It has an unusual force about it. Like a magnet, it attracts more to it. It's bizarre but sit down and think about it. When you have no money you really don't have any, but once you start making money, hopefully it will attract more.

It goes without saying that a depressed and negative outlook on life, espaecially wealth, will definitely work against you. If you have no money but have a positive frame of mind, you can look forward to making money. But a negative outlook will almost certainly stifle any creativity or moneymaking ideas you have.

Remember you have to start somewhere and anywhere is better than nowhere, but ensure it's an ethical start. Making money from criminal proceeds or by harming others is the wrong way to start out. It's not only unethical but your wealth status will be loaded with negative energy and will most likely come back to 'haunt' you.

In this book we have seen how wealth takes on a specific meaning. It is not the material possessions you own, but the financial assets you have that are important. Your wardrobe of designer clothes may look good, but in real terms is worth very little. Had you paid that money into a savings account, it would have attracted some interest and

Having respect for money is essential. If you can't respect it, it won't respect you

TOP TIP

that pool of money would have probably grown in real terms.

You may be asking, why do some people have the ability to make money? Conversely, why do some people with high wages or income never accumulate wealth and yet other people with lesser wages manage to accumulate great wealth? Learn to apply the lessons of this book honestly and openly to your life and you will find the answers to these questions.

Millionaires pay particular attention to their lifestyle and their spending habits. Many millionaires are not phased by their wealth. They do not spend extravagantly and do not own hundreds and hundreds of designer accessories. You will be surprised how some millionaires live - you probably wouldn't even know someone was a millionaire by looking at them. They don't even drive flashy cars.

Some years back I remember going to the market and came across an old woman who was struggling carrying so many bags she was almost invisible behind the bags. She wasn't wearing swanky posh clothes nor did she look like a celebrity. I helped her with the bags and walked her to the bus stop. We established good rapport. Later I found out she was a multi-millionaire! So you see appearances can indeed be deceiving.

On another occasion Mr. Hinduja telephoned me one evening and invited me to dinner. I went along to the event and sat down on a chair. Mr. Lakshmi Mittal came and sat down next to me. He was wearing plain shoes and a dressed down suit.

If he had walked down on the street no one would probably recognise him to be one of the richest men in the country. Mr. Mittal is a billionaire but it was heartening to see that he hadn't got carried away with his billionaire status and could attend an event without being followed by an entourage of people and didn't have to wear a designer label just to prove his status. Both Mr. Mittal and Mr. Hinduja are down-to-earth successful men who have not lost touch with the world around them.

Chapter 11

Money Oils The Wheels

Unfortunately, many people are conditioned to believe that money is the root of all evil. You must have heard people saying, 'Money can't buy you love', or 'What's the point, you can't take it to the grave with you'? They probably mean well. But let's get real the truth is, money makes the world go round, and it can definitely enhance the quality of your lifestyle and that of others.

Don't feel dirty or greedy because you want to make money. When you are intent on becoming rich, you need to ask yourself why you want to be rich. Is it because you want to become financially independent, or is it because you want more money to buy new things? Is it because you want to buy expensive household goods? Or is it because you want the zeroes to increase in your bank account? What is your driving force? The answers should tell you a lot of about yourself and your motives.

Perhaps you grew up in a lower-working-class environment. You have done really well. Maybe you went to university and secured a good job. You might be thinking of getting married, or of sharing the same household as your partner. You may have your sights set on a nice house in a wealthy middle-class area, because all your well-to-do friends live in that neighborhood.

Family and peers might be putting on pressure to move up-town, as that would be evidence of your success and wealth. Because of various pressures, you move and take out a large mortgage. You then spend money to fit in with the crowd. Perhaps they go on expensive holidays, and your family wants to do the same thing. Yes, it can be difficult to save especially if you live a high consumption lifestyle.

For instance, you may be a high-flying barrister or a consultant. If so, you may be living in an affluent middle-class neighborhood. Your friends wear designer clothes. They drive top-of-the-range cars and entertain in expensive restaurants. They have expensive tastes and talk about fancy toys.

There may be pressure on you to conform to the same lifestyle. You might feel overwhelmed by the debts that you and your family have. These could range from credit cards to mortgage and hire purchase agreements. If you're the main breadwinner in the household, you may feel, 'I don't even know where to begin!'

> Once you are rich you have the luxury of employing the best brains in the business.
>
> **TOP TIP**

Take a break. Have a look at the vicious circle you are in. They say poverty is a vicious cycle, but as you move up the ladder another cycle eats your wealth.

Don't get me wrong. It doesn't mean you have to become a Scrooge. But what you don't have to do is spend foolishly on material possessions that you don't really need.

When this is the case, it could really pay to sit down with your partner and work out how much money both of you are earning and saving. Some households have more than one breadwinner. Have a look at what your partner earns. Even if one partner earns less than the other, this is not an excuse not to save. Many people do not realise it, but their own family members may have the power also to share in the dream of becoming rich.

For instance, you may have an income of £40,000 per year while the job your spouse holds brings in £12,000 a year. Together your household income is £52,000. When you budget jointly, you can make cost-effective decisions jointly. Why not open a joint savings account where you save X amount of money every month? As this pool of money grows, you can then invest it appropriately to realise more money.

Find something that you are good at, interested in or passionate about. If you enjoy what you do it's more likely that you will make money from it. Also stay in your lower-end neighborhood, and buy property with a lower mortgage, leaving you with more money to save and invest. A mortgage is not necessarily a bad thing. Your property is an investment. It will realise equity at some stage.

This is not to say that there isn't a chance that the value of your investment might go down. But depending on market conditions, you could make a tidy profit. So it can be a good thing to get on the property ladder. However, don't make the mistake of volunteering to take a high mortgage. If you move to a wealthy neighborhood, you could end up spending money on an expensive car and clothes simply because your environment influences you to do so.

Home is not the only place where expectations can push you over the limit. The work environment can pressurise you to conform and spend. For instance, if you work in a multi-million pound complex in a city environment, there may be added pressure to buy the finest bespoke suits because the clients expect it, or drive the latest car for the same kind of reason. Indeed, there is the potential that you may lose business if you do not. That's OK. You just need to find another strategy. Buy suits, but buy them during the sales; you are more likely to pick up a bargain.

> As you save and your wealth grows your confidence and outlook on life will change, hopefully for the better.
>
> **TOP TIP**

Learn to look after your clothes. Get into habit of caring for them as they will last longer. For instance, get them pressed, and hang them in your wardrobe to withstand the effect of creases and early wear and tear.

If you are part of a high-spending lifestyle group, you may eat away at your money through engaging in social activities. Perhaps your friends are members of expensive golf clubs, gyms, and sports centres. If you are a member of several centres, downsize! Don't be one of those people who hold memberships without ever participating in the activities of the club or rarely using them.

In the end, those people who shine brightest and make the greatest impact are those with an inner belief in their personal right to the happiness and prosperity that being confident brings. Life situations can change dramatically when someone who is immensely confident enters the picture.

There is no need to be loud, or to bring attention to yourself through public stunts. When you believe strongly in yourself, you will exude confidence. It will manifest itself in everything you do, from the way you shake someone's hand, to the way you walk, and the way you enter any building. The effects are amazing.

You will be successful because that is the only course your life can take, barring an untimely meeting with fate. When you believe something with a passion, it is bound to come true because its pursuit will become second nature. Therefore, the belief that you can and will become a millionaire is the most important aspect of this journey. Unless you make this affirmation, you will not take the steps necessary to realise your millionaire potential.

Setbacks that are only temporary in nature will become permanent if they set up camp in your psyche, where they will definitely stifle your chances of success. Confidence in your ability to become a millionaire will not make you a millionaire. However, it will take you a lot closer. On the contrary, a lack of confidence is about as sure a sign of defeat as a white flag of surrender.

If you have a passion to make money and live comfortably then really aim to do that and do it well. Invest your time and efforts in achieving your aim. Just imagine when you do start becoming wealthy you can invest the money in appreciable assets that will work for you 24 hours a day, 7 days a week, 52 weeks in the year, every year.

Stop buying on credit. It's a sure way to lose wealth.

TOP TIP

So even when you are actually asleep something is still making money for you. Wouldn't you love to be in that position? Indeed all the millionaires I have spoken to have appreciable assets they are still making money while they are sleeping!

As you continue through this book, you are probably beginning to realise that becoming wealthy is easier than you thought. And that alone will give you confidence. The motivation to make sufficient funds for investment, links closely to your current source of income your occupation. Clearly, if you hate your job, you will not be motivated to do it satisfactorily and this will obviously effect your motivation to save and subsequently invest.

A common characteristic of self-made millionaires is a deep and ingrained love for what they do. There are few things more fulfilling to a self-made millionaire than the daily conducting of business. Your occupation should be something you look forward to each day, and not something you consider as five days of punishment with a two-day rest period. The importance of occupying yourself with an occupation you enjoy and its connection with the ultimate goal of becoming a millionaire, is obvious.

As human beings, we usually perform better at something we enjoy. Therefore, we are more likely to reap the fruits of success in the form of promotions, raises, stock options, and other benefits of work done at a very high level. It follows that we then have more money to save and to invest.

Some see these financial increases as opportunities to get yet another Mercedes or that expensive suit seen on a stroll down Saville Row. However, the individual with the millionaire mindset views these manifestations of success on the job in terms of making the funds work for him or her.

This may include channelling the savings towards investment. This does not mean that you can spend none of your newly acquired funds on anything other than that which will make you money. What it does mean is that saving will be the primary focus and the acquisition of treats will be secondary. It is very difficult to motivate yourself when you view the path to earning those funds for financial independence as a prison sentence.

Chapter 12

What Really Turns You On

YES, THAT'S SOMETHING you need to get really clear about. Learn about how you respond to life's challenges. Begin right here. Learn to think like a millionaire. Get the millionaire mind-set and you can make money. READ THIS BOOK 2-3 TIMES until you are absolutely sure that you have grasped the secrets of wealth building.

You can make a huge amount of money if you believe in your dream or enjoy the work YOU ARE IN. Learn to save. Sit down and get this simple concept into your head. Once you understand it, you can teach this to your children and siblings. It will help them understand the rules for making money. If you tend to spend more than you save, you need to make some serious cutbacks.

And that means they will already be looking at the underlying issues that belong in relationships, because the two go together. Other people are a resource, just like money is. When you appreciate the meaning of income, you will realise that this is money coming in, for instance your monthly salary.

Most people have some sort of income. Less wealthy

people only have one type of income. This is normally their weekly or monthly wage. When your expenses and liabilities are very high, you need to do some urgent downsizing, but when your assets are higher than your liabilities, you are already on the road to financial success.

Make a list of the sources of your income. Wealthy people have several types of income. This could include money coming from real estate, from shares, and from other sources, such as insurance royalties. Also there may be a second income coming into your household and you may not realise it. Your spouse/partner may be earning, but not effectively contributing to the household wealth building.

Learn not to accumulate liabilities. These include bank loans, credit cards, hire-purchase agreements, and related products. These will eat away your wealth.

When you go shopping, are you happy when buying food and other items using a card? I bet you don't even know sometimes how much the spree cost you. It's tempting and easy to pay by plastic. But when you pay by cash, at least you know what you are paying for.

If you own lots of credit cards, cut them up. If you really can't do without one, keep just one. You don't need lots of them. It's better to pay cash. That way you can appreciate that you are spending money and you tend to stop and think before you spend. Plastic is the great curse of

Health is wealth. Wealth is health.

TOP TIP

contemporary living. Getting into the cash habit, it has the potential to save you thousands of pounds.

Also, the moment you start spending to 'fit in' with others (i.e. keeping up with the 'Jones'), then that is the moment your wealth will begin to dissipate. So be careful before you start to spend, spend, spend. The avenue through which to realise the dream of becoming a millionaire begins with saving and ends with investing.

You need to eat and live, so expenses relating to food and mortgage expenses are OK. But do pay particular attention to those other, hidden expenses that you can cut back on. Answer these questions truthfully. Do you spend a lot of money socialising? On alcohol? On clothes? You can actually save money when you can discipline yourself a little. Keep your eyes open for bargains and opportunities wherever you go.

Do you smoke tobacco? It is an increasingly expensive habit. Maybe it's time you seriously considered giving up cigarettes so that you can save money. Think of all the spare cash you could have. There are a variety of clinics and products on the market that can help you cut out these addictive habits that can eat away at your wealth.

When you work for a company/organisation, you are not only working for your employer but ALSO working for the taxman and the bank. They will take money OUT of your pay packet BEFORE you have access to it. However, when you are wealthy, you pay YOURSELF FIRST, then the taxman and bank. Work out where you fit in this scenario.

Even people whose earnings are in the highest category may still accumulate very little wealth. This relates both to a high-consumption lifestyle and to the astronomical amount of tax charged against their income. Yes, you do have to pay out, but consider other ways of minimising your tax liability. The first step is absurdly simple. Get yourself a good accountant or financial adviser. And also invest in good accounts software that is user-friendly and which will help you keep track of your expenses and outgoings. Unless you keep an eye on your spending habits, you can't make savings. If you don't have access to a computer, at least start the habit of keeping a record by hand of your outgoings, savings, expenses and so forth.

Part of learning to maximise your income potential to create and generate wealth is to use tax knowledge for your own benefit. Rich people pay fewer taxes, while those who are not wealthy pay out their money first to the Inland Revenue department, and then to their banks. Contrast that with the rich, who pay themselves first. You can charge

> If you are successful in making money you will become successful in all areas of your life.
>
> **TOP TIP**

the expense of using an accountant against your tax bill. He will know all about tax laws that could work for you, and which you have a right to use to save yourself money. Assets have the promise of generating money. They add to your wealth portfolio. Being wealthy is not about how much money you have, per se, but how much you are actually worth. When calculating your worth for example add the value of your home (equity) to your shares and stocks, rental income, and so on.

Buying a lottery ticket, betting on horses and dogs at races and poker are not routes to becoming rich. They can become dangerous addictions and habits. The promise of making huge amounts of wealth is there, but very often you lose money, not make it. Be careful where and how you spend your money.

Wealthy people raise money from their existing assets to purchase property with cash, thereby saving money on excessive mortgage interest payments. Moreover, they cover expenses from the funds they make from their assets. But don't be discouraged. A house retains its equity, and when the market place is booming, you can always sell and release that equity and invest it to make more money. In fact, Buying and selling properties could make you a millionaire in a few years. But interest rates can go up and down. And who can forget the recession of the '80s when the market crashed and the value of property was wiped out overnight as interest rates hit sky-high records. So be careful.

The traditional image of millionaires is very dated. They are becoming wealthier much earlier in their lives. It is also a fact that many of the millionaires are of Asian origin. The healthy state of the stock market and information technology, including the Internet, has helped make millionaires into multi-millionaires.

So where do you fit in this picture? If you are going to buy a house, buy something you can manage. Don't start with a massive mortgage especially if you can't keep up with the huge mortgage payments. You need something manageable. Don't be forced into a wealthy neighborhood just because you think that will be evidence of your high status.

Often, people take on big mortgages and then spend all their time trying to keep up with payments. This means they have no additional funds to invest. Wealthy people generally tend to live below their means and spend money wisely. They accumulate wealth through persistent hard work. If they can do it, why can't you?

When you have wealth you are in a powerful position you have much more control of your life and your destiny.

TOP TIP

Millionaires are:

- Financially independent
- Financially literate
- Avid investors and savers
- Meticulous about avoiding an extravagant lifestyle.
- Homeowners
- Their own bosses
- Responsible for planning and budgeting their finances

When you are serious about making money, are you ready and able to change your lifestyle? It may be difficult, in the short term. Cutting back and saving now will bring financial security in the long run.

The financial assets you own, not by the clothes you wear define wealth. Net worth is how you define someone who is wealthy - it means your current assets, less your liabilities.

Another way to define and establish whether you are wealthy depends on your income and age. The younger you are, the more time you have to make money. The higher your income bracket, the more likely you can accumulate wealth. However, your income bracket does NOT always define your wealth.

For instance, when you earn £60,000 but spend £50,000 of that every year, then you only have £10,000 spare for investment. Conversely, you may earn £25,000 and save £15,000. In this case, you already have the mind-set of a millionaire. Savings and being frugal are the key ingredients to becoming a millionaire.

Some people are born with a silver spoon in their mouth. That saying often describes millionaires who have inherited wealth, as opposed to self-made ones. When you are in the first group, that's great. It's not your fault you inherited it. Nonetheless, be aware that you're lucky to be in that position. What are you going to do with it? The same rules apply to you as they do to the person who has inherited nothing. Stay motivated, learn to invest wisely, and quadruple what you already have.

If you fall into the second group, don't be disheartened.

Continuing education is the key to lifetime success.

TOP TIP

You can still become a millionaire. At least 25% of Americans fall into the second group. Bill Gates alone has as much wealth as the bottom 40% of U.S. households. Recent figures suggest that the UK's millionaires could now populate a city.

There is many a story of millionaires who have become bankrupt and lost all their money. Learn from their mistakes. Mr. Varma, one of the cleverest and shrewdest millionaires I have come across, says when you are extremely successful, the bank will offer you endless money and is like an umbrella. But when the rain comes, i.e. when you are experiencing difficulties in business, the bank will most probably take back the umbrella! Moral: don't rely on your bank for everything! They will let you down when you really need them. That's the advice many millionaires have given me. The bank should be your last resort.

The speed with which information technology is moving means the world is truly your oyster. You don't have to limit your business and services to the country where you live.

This is the age of the worldwide web. It's a place where we have the luxury of doing business, sourcing, and investing throughout the world over the Internet, through email, and so on. This is a great time to go out and make money.

Chapter 13

Top Tips

It's never too late to start your aim of becoming a millionaire. There is no age limit!

TOP TIP

Find a role model and emulate them!

TOP TIP

This is a fertile time to make money!

TOP TIP

"A journey begins with a single step" (Chinese proverb)!

TOP TIP

Look for non-traditional routes to make money!

TOP TIP

To make a million, you need a strategy. Just as a barber needs a scissors to cut hair, so too there are certain tools that the wannabe millionaire needs!

TOP TIP

You have to believe you can make money. If you think like a failure then you will become one!

TOP TIP

The world is becoming 'smaller' and this is a perfect time to make money!

TOP TIP

Millionaires love investing whether its passion, love, time or money!

TOP TIP

Use feng shui to attract wealth!

TOP TIP

Learn to work with the energy field that surrounds you!

TOP TIP

Create a harmonious working environment!

TOP TIP

Stagnated qi (energy) can lead to bad fortune!

TOP TIP

A round table as opposed to one with harsh straight lines can be more conducive to business meetings!

TOP TIP

Light deprivation can affect your mood negatively!

TOP TIP

Improving customer staff relations will help increase your profits!

TOP TIP

If you want to make money in business you need trained staff!

TOP TIP

Two goldfish in a bowl can attract positive energy into your life and business!

TOP TIP

Colour therapy can be used to generate wealth!

TOP TIP

Some of the most successful companies have attracted customers (and wealth) simply by changing their environment.

TOP TIP

If you want to make money in business you need trained staff who know how to treat customers and clients with courtesy. Otherwise you may lose the customer!

TOP TIP

You can become a millionaire by tapping into the power of your mind!

TOP TIP

Visualize how your mega-million pound/dollar empire will ultimately look. Use positive images to achieve your aim!

TOP TIP

Aside from banks, take a look around for other sources for loans!

TOP TIP

Foster the belief that in your mind 'I will become a millionaire' watch how you start to accumulate wealth!

TOP TIP

If your brainwaves are unbalanced you will not make money!

TOP TIP

Get into the cash habit and cut down on credit. Credit is one of the ugliest monsters created!

TOP TIP

Tap into the wealth file in your brain using yoga and make money!

TOP TIP

You won't make money if you believe it is inherently 'evil'!

TOP TIP

Improve your concentration and unleash your creative powers!

TOP TIP

Being grounded and calm helps produce better quality work!

TOP TIP

Learn to access your mental money file!

TOP TIP

Keep on top of current financial affairs as well as a keen eye on the economic markets, latest trends and new ideas!

TOP TIP

Learn to save, save, save!

TOP TIP

Millionaires accept risks and responsibilities. Making money is not for cowards or thieves!

TOP TIP

Investigate how many incomes come into your household. Combine incomes to generate wealth quickly!

TOP TIP

Avoid an extravagant lifestyle!

TOP TIP

Self-employed people have a better chance statistically of becoming millionaires!

TOP TIP

Calculate in advance what you expect to spend each month. Budget wisely!

TOP TIP

Poor management will cripple any business you set up and/or prevent it from achieving success!

TOP TIP

Poor quality staff cost you more money in the long run. Poor results, less productivity and complaints will follow, in time!

TOP TIP

Watch your competitors!

TOP TIP

You can generate wealth from projects you actually 'enjoy' doing!

TOP TIP

There is no time to be resting. When you die, you will sleep forever!

TOP TIP

Learn basic accounting skills!

TOP TIP

Keep your eyes open for bargains and learn to barter and haggle!

TOP TIP

Key ingredients to becoming wealthy include a strong work ethic!

TOP TIP

Be prepared to sacrifice your leisure time!

TOP TIP

Don't be afraid to take risks!

TOP TIP

Millionaires get wholeheartedly behind the product or service they are offering and this motivates them to make more money!

TOP TIP

Don't be lazy!

TOP TIP

Have a plan - it will save you time and money!

TOP TIP

Establish whether there is a client base for your target audience!

TOP TIP

Brush up your creative skills you will need plenty of them to make money!

TOP TIP

Stop buying on credit. It's a sure way to lose wealth!

TOP TIP

Invest in your health!

TOP TIP

If you are successful in making money you will become successful in all areas of your life!

TOP TIP

Continuing education is the key to lifetime success!

TOP TIP

Making a million is always difficult. But once you have made that first million the ride is easy!

TOP TIP

Learn the meaning of the following words: asset, expense, liability, equity, saving!

TOP TIP

Keep a record of your spending and investing habits and you will spot opportunities to build wealth!

TOP TIP

Detox regularly and eat healthily - purify your mind and body!

TOP TIP

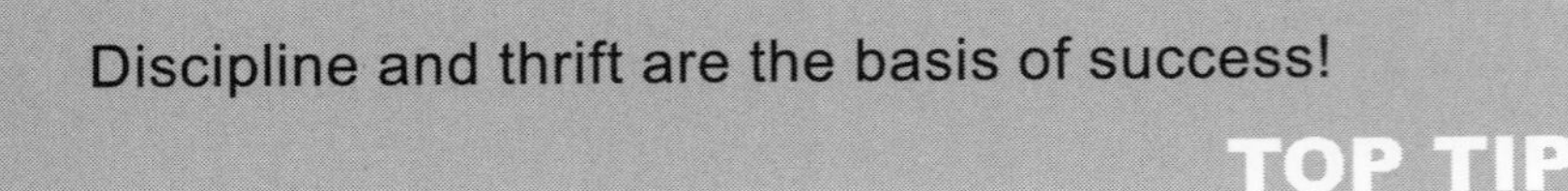

Don't blame your circumstances - get on with life!

TOP TIP

Millionaires 'pull the strings' they employ other people to work for them!

TOP TIP

Decide what your long-term priorities are!

TOP TIP

De-clutter your mind!

TOP TIP

Stay organized!

TOP TIP

Keep the company of positively minded people!

TOP TIP

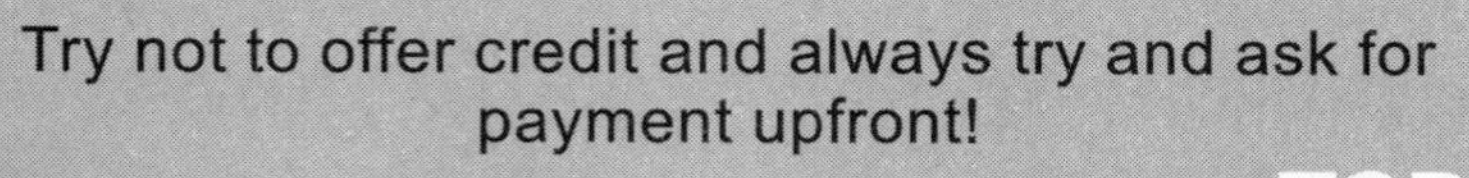

Don't give up on the first sign of trouble. Perseverance is the key!

TOP TIP

Pay particular attention to your lifestyle!

TOP TIP

You may need to sacrifice your leisure activities when you are on the route to making a million!

TOP TIP

Money is a form of 'energy'!

TOP TIP

Money attracts money!

TOP TIP

Live below your means!

TOP TIP

Aim high and believe in your ability to generate wealth!

TOP TIP

Establish what your long-term priorities are!

TOP TIP

Stay focused!

TOP TIP

Invest in assets that make money for you 24-7 even while you are sleeping!

TOP TIP

Get into the cash habit!

TOP TIP

Thrift and discipline are key ingredients for making money!

TOP TIP

Time is precious - use it wisely!

TOP TIP

"Money is like muck: not good unless it is spread"
(Francis Bacon)!

TOP TIP

Aside from banks look around for other sources for loans to help set you up in business. If you can't set up a business then go self-employed!

TOP TIP

Protect your assets. You could lose money paying out huge sums in legal costs through divorce, business partnerships or even personal injury claims!

TOP TIP

Don't work to spend - work to save!

TOP TIP

If you have children of your own - teach them maths!

TOP TIP

Aim high. Don't limit your ambitions or dreams. You have one shot at this life go for it anything is possible nothing is impossible. Life is what you make it!

TOP TIP

To make money eat well and healthy.

TOP TIP

"Making a million has always been difficult. Making a million illegally has always been a little easier. Keeping a million when you have made it is perhaps the most difficult of all."
(Jeffrey Archer)

If you are running a business and have inefficient, rude, untrustworthy, obnoxious staff, just remember you are losing money invisibly!

TOP TIP

Aside from banks, take a look around for other potential sources for help to start up your business, for instance EC funding or a partnership with a like minded person!

TOP TIP

"Maya Ko Milay, Maya Kar Kar Lambay Hath"
Money makes money. Money attracts money
(Tulsi Das Ancient Indian
Poet and philosopher)!

TOP TIP

High consumption families tend to spend money on material goods. Change your and your family's lifestyles!

TOP TIP

You can only make money if others make it for you!

TOP TIP

As you save and your wealth grows your confidence and outlook on life will change, hopefully for the better!

TOP TIP

Health is wealth. Wealth is health!

TOP TIP

When you have wealth you are in a powerful position you have much more control of your life and your destinies!

TOP TIP

"Early to rise, early to bed makes a man (or woman) healthy, wealthy and wise" (Old English saying)!

TOP TIP

Learn to meditate. This will greatly improve your powers of concentration and stamina.

TOP TIP

Being grounded and calm helps produce better quality work!

TOP TIP

Improve your concentration and unleash your creative powers!

TOP TIP

Learn to access your mental money file!

TOP TIP

If you control the subconscious mind you can become rich!

TOP TIP

You have the power to remove data that is harmful, negative, corrupted and illogical and which is stored in the subconscious mind!

TOP TIP

Practicing yoga can help you become rich. It also improves brain power, levels of concentration, stamina, confidence and delay the onset of ageing!

TOP TIP

Yoga technology is a blue-print for living!

TOP TIP

By practising yoga you can release toxins that are the root of the negative static charge which is preventing you from making money!

TOP TIP

Meditation and related practices not only still the mind but also help to unleash your creative potential!

TOP TIP

Money is a powerful weapon - use it wisely!

TOP TIP

Money is energy - learn to tap into this 'energy'!

TOP TIP